YELLOW NOTEBOOK

PRAISE FOR HELEN GARNER

'This is the power of Garner's writing. She drills into experience and comes up with such clean, precise distillations of life, once you read them they enter into you. Successive generations of writers have felt the keen influence of her work and for this reason Garner has become part of us all.' *Australian*

'Garner is a natural storyteller.' James Wood, *New Yorker*

'Her prose is wiry, stark, precise, but to find her equal for the tone of generous humanity one has to call up writers like Isaac Babel and Anton Chekhov.' *Wall Street Journal*

'Helen Garner [is] our greatest contemporary practitioner of observation, self-interrogation and compassion. Everything she writes, in her candid, graceful prose, rings true, enlightens, stays.' Joan London

'Her use of language is sublime.' *Scotsman*

'Garner's stories share characteristics of the postcard: they flash before us carefully recorded images that remind us of harsher realities not pictured. And like postcards they are economically written, a bit of conversation is transcribed, a memory recalled, an event noted, scenes pass as if viewed from a train—momentarily, distinct and tantalising in their beauty.' *New York Times*

'There's no denying the force of her storytelling.' *Telegraph*

'Garner is one of those wonderful writers whose voice one hears and whose eyes one sees through. Her style, conversational but never slack, is natural, supple and exact, her way of seeing is acute and sympathetic, you receive an instant impression of being in the company of a congenial friend and it is impossible not to follow her as she brings to life the events and feelings she is exploring.' Diana Athill

'A voice of great honesty and energy.' Anne Enright

'Scrupulously objective and profoundly personal.' Kate Atkinson

'Garner's spare, clean style flowers into magnificent poetry.' *Australian Book Review*

'She has a Jane Austen–like ability to whizz an arrow straight into the truest depths of human nature, including her own.' *Life Sentence*

'Compassionate and dispassionate in equal measure…She writes with a profound understanding of human vulnerability, and of the subtle workings of love, memory and remorse.' *Economist*

'Garner's precise descriptions, her interest in minute shifts of emotion, and the ways in which we reveal ourselves to others are always at work in these books, and make them a real joy to read.' *Age*

'She watches, imagines, second-guesses, empathises, agonises. Her voice—intimate yet sharp, wry yet urgent—inspires trust.' *Atlantic*

'Garner's writing [is] so assured and compassionate that any reader will be enthralled and swept along.' *Books+Publishing*

'The words almost dance off the page.' *Launceston Examiner*

'Garner is a beautiful writer who winkles out difficult emotions from difficult hiding places.' *Sunday Telegraph*

'Garner writes with a fearsome, uplifting grace.' *Metro UK*

'A combination of wit and lyricism that is immensely alluring.' *Observer*

'Honest, unsparing and brave.' *New York Times*

ALSO BY HELEN GARNER

FICTION
Monkey Grip
Honour & Other People's Children
The Children's Bach
Postcards from Surfers
Cosmo Cosmolino
The Spare Room
Stories

NON-FICTION
The First Stone
The Feel of Steel
Joe Cinque's Consolation
This House of Grief
Everywhere I Look
True Stories

FILM SCRIPTS
The Last Days of Chez Nous
Two Friends

HELEN GARNER
YELLOW NOTEBOOK
DIARIES VOLUME I 1978–1987

TEXT PUBLISHING
MELBOURNE AUSTRALIA

textpublishing.com.au

The Text Publishing Company
Swann House, 22 William Street, Melbourne Victoria 3000, Australia

The Text Publishing Company (UK) Ltd
130 Wood Street, London EC2V 6DL, United Kingdom

Copyright © Helen Garner 2019

The moral right of Helen Garner to be identified as the author of this work has been asserted.

All rights reserved. Without limiting the rights under copyright above, no part of this publication shall be reproduced, stored in or introduced into a retrieval system, or transmitted in any form or by any means (electronic, mechanical, photocopying, recording or otherwise), without the prior permission of both the copyright owner and the publisher of this book.

Published by The Text Publishing Company, 2019.

Book design by W. H. Chong.
Jacket photograph by William Yang.
Typeset by J&M Typesetting.

Printed in Australia by Griffin Press, an accredited ISO/NZS 14001:2004 Environmental Management System printer.

ISBN: 9781922268143 (hardback)
ISBN: 9781925774917 (ebook)

A catalogue record for this book is available from the National Library of Australia.

 This book is printed on paper certified against the Forest Stewardship Council® Standards. Griffin Press holds FSC chain-of-custody certification SGS-COC-005088. FSC promotes environmentally responsible, socially beneficial and economically viable management of the world's forests.

'We are here for this—to make mistakes and to correct ourselves, to stand the blows and hand them out.'
PRIMO LEVI, *The Periodic Table*

1978

Maybe it'd be a good idea to start another diary, just to cream it off. I bought this yellow book today.

―――

Man in the metro, a 1950s relic but *real*, not an affectation—untidy, perfectly period clothes—lumber jacket, tight trousers, big, worn, nondescript shoes. He was playing an exquisite basic rock-and-roll guitar and singing 'Corinna' through a little amp that looked like a white Daisy Duck radio.

―――

Monkey Grip appears to have won the National Book Council Award. Letter from T in Melbourne: 'Sometimes I fall into the trap of thinking that jobs and money and grants are luck instead of recognition for talent and hard work. Do you feel that still?'

―――

I know what the matter is. I haven't got any women friends here. I miss, I miss. I feel crazy and weepy.

―――

F says he's not really French: that he comes from the south, that it's different there. He says if you don't turn a mattress it starts to smell bad. He sings to himself as he works. If he looks over my shoulder at this I'll start screaming.

Actually, I don't care if he reads this. I'm protected by the fog of incomprehension that's always between us unless we work single-mindedly at *direct contact*.

   M and I work to wall off a sleeping space for her at one end of the living room. We stretch a length of unbleached calico tightly over the back of the high, open shelf we bought at Habitat, stand it at right angles to the wall, then lie side by side on her little bed and gaze at the tent-like structure. A bottle of Scotch on the living-room side picks up the light and shines a brown glow through the fabric. When we do a task together she turns me into a better mother. She's a witty person, companionable and kind. 'Got any idea how to draw a hamster?'

Rilke wrote that when people know your name they 'scatter your forces'. He suggests changing your name as soon as they get hold of it.

I must disabuse myself of the illusion that I once sat down and wrote a novel. I am not good at constructing major pieces of work. I have a short concentration span. I can work only in small, intense bursts. I don't seem to work consciously. I write to unburden myself, to amuse myself, to arrange in order the things that bulge in my head, to make myself notice things.

Jerzy Kosiński's absolutely unemotional style. As clear as crystal, as objects arranged in a line. Whenever the lost child in *The Painted Bird* approaches a farm to ask for work or for shelter, the peasants 'consult their neighbours'.

At Cap Fréhel F tried to stop me from tackling the cliff. 'Don't climb!' he cried, white-faced, seizing my ankle. So as not to watch me, he went to prise mussels off the rocks with his knife. I climbed. His fear had infected me. The void sucked at my back.

———

I have a lot of trouble with self-disgust. It disgusts me that I repeat things in this book that I have already written in letters. It disgusts me that I am so lazy.

———

A critic in Melbourne writes that 'some people consider *Monkey Grip*'s subject matter distasteful'. Someone else said I was a traitor to my class. I now grasp the meaning of the term *provincial*.

———

Cure for homesickness and ennui: walk. I must have walked ten kilometres yesterday. Bought two jumpers and a pair of red shoes, which are perfect.

———

I went to shake hands with Solange. She laughed and went 'Oh!' as if to say 'Come off it!' and kissed my cheeks instead.

———

M didn't understand the information the teacher gave about the week's holiday for Toussaint: she thought it was a school camp, and tried to ask if she was supposed to bring her sleeping bag and something to eat. The teacher had no idea what she was talking about. M gave up and came home bewildered. She cried when she tried to explain to me what had happened.

———

Drank some kir and this and that. In Charlie Hebdo I read: 'BOUM! = NO FUTURE x 7.' I laughed and laughed. I don't even know why it's funny. If I lived alone with my leedle cassette player and idiosyncratic assortment of tapes, I'd probably drink myself stupid.

———

F took an old wooden-handled hammer out of his briefcase this morning and laid it on my desk. It's still there.

How he pronounces VAPORUB.

We went walking in the cold, up to Place Clichy and rue Joseph de Maistre etc. He put his hand through my arm and I was happy.

The visitor on his way to London—'It's my spiritual home!'—spoke about his poems as being ahead of their time. 'In ten years people will see what I was trying to do.' I doubt this. Also, he was too cheap to pay fifty centimes to use the toilet at Parc Monceau.

I wish I lived peacefully somewhere. I wish I had a shit job involving physical exertion.

In Toulouse our hostess made a dormitory of her bedroom and she, M and I slept comfortably in a row. All the sheets and towels, from her trousseau sixteen years ago, are embroidered with her initials. At about 4 pm I remembered that it was my birthday. She took us out of the city to stay with some friends in a village. On the drive she told us that the husband had had an affair. The wife had fought it, or sat it out. He had returned to her. 'So,' she said with a satisfaction that did not quite convince me, 'she won.' The air in the house was thick. The husband and wife did not look at each other. In the afternoon we walked halfway up a small mountain. An easy track. Chestnuts still bright with yellow leaves. At night the darkness and silence around the house frightened me.

A drunk black man in a cobbled street yelled at us that we were *'de la pourriture'*.

Tweezers. Wool. Needles. Pencil sharpener.

A certain graciousness of manner; a deep courtesy.

'I'll be the toughest kid in the whereabouts,' says M.

'The fact that the glass is raised to the lips without being smashed into the face is a tribute to the subtle weighing abilities of the outstretched limb. And the fact that the glass remains at the mouth while losing weight as it is emptied shows how punctually the news is updated: without this information the glass would levitate as it was drained.' —Jonathan Miller

Some teargas got in my eyes at the demo. It was my first dose, unbelievably confusing and painful. I was surprised at how philosophical people were about it. They covered their noses and mouths. '*Aii*!' said F's friend. 'It hurts your eyes! Well, that's what it's for, I suppose.' Everyone around him laughed.

Despair and sadness and fear are easier to write about than hope, happiness, confidence.

Middlemarch. A substance smooth of surface but containing firm lumps of foreign matter.

The famous publisher and his translator took me to lunch at Brasserie Lipp. I am sure they will not want my book. They addressed me in perfect English. They were unbearably chic. When I offered my hand to the translator, all she gave me was her little finger. My cheeks were red with awkwardness. She worked hard, I suppose:

'See the man with the moustache? That's Romain Gary.'

'He looks sad,' I said.

'He's been looking like that ever since Jean Seberg left him.'

———

F is sick. I'm looking after him. He hates to be *'dépendant'*, but he appears to have abandoned attempts to fight it and is sitting up in my bed reading *Playboy France*.

———

M cries because I get eight letters and she gets only a postcard. She refuses to speak to me, then bursts into tears, casts herself on to my lap, and sobs: 'I had a sudden feeling of meanness.' In the afternoon we sit together knitting. She is so thrilled about her new cherry-red knee-high boots that she can hardly sleep. Soon after midnight I wake to find her standing beside my bed, fully dressed for school: 'I thought it was morning!'

———

I quarrelled with F because I wouldn't show him a fan letter I was writing to Woody Allen. He says that he and his former girlfriend used to show each other everything. He says I'm secretive. It's strange to realise that I am a very different person from the one I thought I was.

———

Siouxsie and the Banshees at l'Empire. They were revolting.

———

Divorce papers came today from Australia. I was sad, remembering that failure, afraid of another one, of being unable to go on loving someone eminently worthy of love. 'Love is your last chance. There is really nothing else on earth to keep you there.' —Louis Aragon, quoted by Patrick White in *A Fringe of Leaves*

———

It was snowing at Père Lachaise. My sister in a pink beret, long blue coat, pink scarf. We picked our way between the graves looking for Proust's. A frozen jonquil lay on his shiny black tombstone. A dark day, very still and cold. Tomorrow she's taking M home to Melbourne.

———

We didn't cry at the airport. She was excited to be travelling home to her father with her groovy aunt. I got back to the dark apartment and tidied up her belongings. That's when I howled, finding the dozens of little half-used notebooks in which she had been obliged to amuse herself drawing and writing because she had no playmates. My girl, stuck in a foreign country with her cranky mother. Is there any point to this guilt? What she learned from being here I can only guess at.

———

I read the paper and doors open in my head like those in a cuckoo clock. I had forgotten why people read papers. You learn things. Ideas come to you. Connections strike off each other with ringing blows or slot together like carpenters' joints.

———

Everyone's talking about *Apocalypse Now*. My work seems piddling, narrow, domestic.

———

I helped F's journalist friend spackle the walls in his new apartment. I was afraid he'd scorn me for my ignorance of politics but when I happened casually to mention Ibsen he looked embarrassed and said, '*Qui ça?*'

———

At the Parc de Bagatelle we had to pay to get in. One franc, fifty. It was worth it. Crocuses and daffodils.

———

M rings from Melbourne: 'Me and my best friend did a show, and the kids applauded really really loudly. Louder than for the other kids who did a play.'

———

Postcard from my sister, a Renoir pencil drawing of a heavy-bodied, half-naked girl reading. A thought balloon: 'Will my shape still be fashionable in the 1970's? Probably not.'

———

F and I took our bikes on the train to the forest of Compiègne and rode along the paths and avenues. Only one squabble. Pale green leaves everywhere. Blue flowers like cloud shimmered in the clearings. A deer bounded across the road in front of us—it came flying from nowhere, struck the ground a single blow with its dainty hooves, and took off again into the trees. In a cafe we raved about it to the barman. He was too bored even to fake interest. We felt foolish and urban; drank up and pedalled away.

———

The film-maker's blue jumper and bright blue eyes. He says that at Cannes people took him for Mick Jagger and asked for his autograph. I never noticed till today that he's rather beautiful. I say 'rather' because he is *affected*, physically. I wonder what he's like when he's alone.

———

I think all the time about the thing I'm supposed to be writing, that I've got a *grant* to be writing. I've found a library to work in. Rue Pavée. If I write what I want to, about the people I know at home, I'll never be able to live in Melbourne again. About the woman who always sang in a register too high for her voice, and that wasn't the worst of it. Lazy, charming G in his band, all the girls hanging round him waiting to be fucked. I don't even do the dishes or cook. I change the position of my bed. I buy huge sheets of drawing paper, pin them to the bedroom wall, cover them with diagrams of characters and their inter-relating. I play the High Rise Bombers tape full-blast and dance by myself, jumping high in the air. Then I crash into appalling bouts of self-doubt, revulsion at my past behaviour, loathing for my emotional habits and the fact that I still feel the need to expose, thinly disguised or barely metamorphosed, my own experience. In the metro this morning, on my way to the library, I felt grey and shrivelled, watching the tunnel lights slip past in their rhythm, wishing that I spoke French twice as well as I do and had a real job with people I didn't particularly like, so I wouldn't have to produce my own raison d'être every day, like a spider yanking thread out of its own guts, or wherever the hell they pull it from.

1979

I've found a workroom I can rent, over a dress shop in Moonee Ponds. It looks north towards a low mountain very far away. In a corner, a hand basin. Its drain is clogged and it's full of old brown water. Maybe mozzies will breed in it. I don't care. I'm writing three sentences a day. Wretched, ill-tempered, nervous, unbearable. Maybe I'm a one-book woman.

―

M brings home a note about the school concert: 'Children should come dressed to the hall. Boys to come in pyjamas. Halos and Wings will be put on by teachers.'

―

HG: (*getting out of the car at 2 am*) 'There's the saucepan.'
    F: 'What?'
    HG: 'See that first star? Go up from there, and further, and there it is.'
    F: 'That is *not* the saucepan.'
    HG: 'For thirty-seven years I have called that star formation "the saucepan". When I was a little girl my father took me by the hand and pointed up and said, "That is the saucepan." You can't *tell me* that's not the saucepan.'

―

M ate a real egg from my sister's chook. It was so rich that she retired to bed groaning and sobbing, and couldn't go to school till 10.30: 'I feel all eggy inside.'

———

M and F found a brown pup at the market. Beautiful, but dumb. Our training methods don't work on her. This morning she took off at the front gate. With me in hot pursuit she bolted, trailing her lead, across four lanes of traffic on Mt Alexander Road. She made it unscathed and wound up cringing on her back under a palm tree, shivering and pissing. As I thundered up to her I realised that what she was running from was *me*.

———

The Italian girl who works in the dress shop is engaged. She tells me that for her trousseau her grandmother has given her a quilt that's 'stuffed with duck leaves'. When she talks I feel like swooning. I could stand on the bottom step and listen to her rave all day.

———

At the Kampuchea Benefit I saw half a dozen people I knew at a table and I was too shy to walk over and say hello. I was *scared* to.

———

'F is very funny,' said one of the guys in the band. 'He's got such a fantastic delivery that you laugh even if you don't understand what he's said.'

———

There was a bird singing in the garden. When I opened the back door it was sitting on the chimney trilling away, but as soon as I appeared it flipped across the vegetable patch to a tree on the other side of the fence, where it threw back its head and sang tune after tune, its little beak open like a pair of scissors.

———

Riding round the corner on to Brunswick Road I change gear

clumsily and the whole bike locks. I get it on to the footpath (F already a yellow dot half a mile away on the freeway bridge) and crouch beside it, helplessly regarding the hub and sprockets. A well-dressed pedestrian in her forties stops beside me. 'Got troubles?' 'It's jammed.' She takes one look and points: 'There—it's stuck there.' The chain is wedged between the smallest sprocket and the white frame. I poke my finger in and wiggle. I seize the chain and yank at it. To my surprise it's got give, and spring—so that's how it works! I jerk it free and fit it on to the correct sprocket. A bunch of tissues appears near my face. 'Thankyou!' 'That's all right,' she says with a cheerful, impersonal smile, and strides away. I wipe my hands on the tissues and shove them into my pocket. Now I know I'm home. My country, right or wrong.

———

Memo: do not drink coffee. It makes me uselessly nervy, even trembly, and engenders baseless optimism about my powers of creation.

1980

I met Frank Moorhouse today in Tamani. He remarked that 'organisation of energy' was a crucial matter. A very nice man. Greying curly hair, massive head—a bullyboy in form but sharp and reserved and intelligent in expression. Very careful about wiping his lips while eating. Two blokes I vaguely knew came in and sat with us. They turned on a Carlton performance: rapid-fire wisecracks about Chomsky, war, politics and corrupt journalism. I wanted to scream. Later Frank bought a bottle of 'good bourbon—seeing as I can afford it'. I walked with him (having trouble keeping up) to his office at the university.

HG: 'I can't stand it when blokes talk like those two. I just wish they'd *shut up*.'

FM: (*mildly*) 'They were high on caffeine, weren't they. It was a coffee thing.'

I passed through the kitchen and saw N at the table with my huge galleys on her knee. She looked up with a laugh and said, 'You're going to be hung, drawn and quartered.' I went away in a panic. This morning she said, 'It's delightful to read. I kept laughing. But you're very hard on the character who's partly you.'

M's entrance exam at University High: a hundred and fifty frightened kids being harangued by an old fart in an academic gown. I saw that her face was white. I was ready to kill. I cried all the way home on the bus and walking down our street. She did not look well as she came out of the exam: strained, pale and slightly vague. She told me all about it, with seriousness. I looked at her skinny little leg muscles in fawn tights and wanted to do terrible violence to someone. She said, 'The maths was *really hard*—you know—"If n equals m times 2", that kind of thing. I nearly cried when I saw some of the questions.' She made a trembling gesture with out-stretched arms. 'I just thought, Oh, no!'

―――

A perfect spring morning: colourless clear sky, luminous at the horizon, faint roar of distant traffic, car window pearled with condensation, power lines and antennae sharply defined in pure air. A tall tree behind the house opposite is thick with creamy blossom. A rooster crows far away towards Westgarth Street. Nothing moves except the odd passing bird.

―――

I was cooking dinner tonight while a couple of hard-line leftie visitors raved on at the kitchen table about an academic they knew who was writing a book on Indo-China.

'In Bangkok,' said the woman, 'he got up to all sorts of stuff he could never do in Australia.'

'What, like fucking prostitutes?' I asked.

'Oh, worse. You know—twelve-year-old virgins.' She laughed. 'The kinds of things he shouldn't really be into, considering where he's at.'

I turned back to the stove.

'Actually,' she went on, in a voice softened by affection, 'he fell in love with the first prostitute he got involved with. He wanted to bring her back to Australia. It was a tragic story, really. He spent a fortune getting her papers and everything, and then she didn't want to go.'

Smart girl.

———

'Once you've used your experience to make something,' said T, 'it takes on a life of its own. It's a bit silly to keep dragging it back to its source.'

———

When I read the writers, particularly the Jews, in *Best American Short Stories* I feel lazy, weak and lacking in *skill*. They will drive and drive, these blokes. What does this mean, for me? It means I must push myself outside what I'm sure of. Take risks.

———

Spring night: black sky speckled with stars, air cool and thickly scented with grass, and the odours of things growing.

———

She says she's writing an essay on the nature of art as myth, myth as the expression of male dominance, myth as *useless to women*.

———

Honour will be out in two weeks. It has several fairly serious typos. I resolve not to look at it any more.

———

Yesterday I felt like burning all my old diaries. I spoke about it to two people, a writer and a photographer. Each replied to this effect: 'You'll be the same person, with the same past, whether you burn them or not.' I decided not to burn anything, but to pack them up and store them somewhere where I can't *get at* them.

———

My eyes are sore, and yesterday my front tooth got chipped while I was eating a Butter Menthol, but is now fixed.

1981

Finished rereading E. M. Forster's *Where Angels Fear to Tread*. I'm sure he had never seen a real baby when he wrote it, but this doesn't matter, it's still marvellous. He is one of the writers I long to meet or write to, and this is one way in which I grasp the fact of death: because I can't. Virginia Woolf is another, despite Pamela Brown's insistence to me that Gertrude Stein was greater.

Went to the State Library looking for *Mourning Becomes Electra*. It wasn't where it should have been so I flipped through V. S. Pritchett's *The Working Novelist*. Fabulous, intelligent, witty without even a tinge of the smartypants. 'The cork-pop of the easy epigram.'

To Dallas Brooks Hall to hear Roger Woodward play Chopin. A stiffly dramatic performance: some very controlled throwing up of the hands. I liked the music but his presence was so intellectual and contained that one might as well have been watching a movie. Little warmth; but in certain pieces his control seemed less rigid, and the left hand rolled almost sexually. In a cafe afterwards a man greeted two guys sitting at the other end of my table. He leaned over them with both hands on the table edge, stiff-armed as a detective, and said that he hadn't liked the concert.

HG: (*butting in*) 'Why?'

Him: 'Because it was *bad*.'

HG: 'Yes, but in what precise ways?'

Him: 'Too many wrong notes. Memory lapses, which offended me. And too cold. Very *Polish* interpretation: holding the beat over into the next bar. When *he* does that it's no good because—Rubenstein, for example, when *he* does it he's still in contact with the basic human thing—Claudio Arrau, too, he messes with things, but you always know he's still really *feeling*.'

Finally he left.

'What a bloody bore,' said one of the men. 'Some people have no an*tenn*ae.' He wriggled his hand in the air above his left ear.

The other said, very politely, 'I was quite interested in what he was saying.'

———

Rumour reaches me that H in Prahran has 'joined the born-again Christians'. This does not surprise me. I rang him tonight. After a relaxed twenty-minute conversation he said, 'Can you keep a secret?'

'Yes.'

'Can you really?'

'Of course.'

'I've gone back to Jesus.

He said it completely without irony or defence. With gladness, really. 'I used to act proud,' he said, 'as if the things I'd hung on to from the New Testament were really things I'd made up myself. I was taking the credit for them.'

———

The *Age* asks me to review Beatrice Faust's book *Women, Sex and Pornography*. I file a piece in dialogue form that I really enjoyed writing. They reject it. Would I please rewrite it as a straight review.

Rage and contempt. Cutting potatoes and onions, I reflect on the pain of rejection, and on how little of it I've had to endure. I think of my CAE students and the way I cheerfully rip into their precious work. I could try to learn a lesson from their humility. I agree to rewrite.

———

Reagan gets shot, but not killed. On TV, the high, thin voice of the gunman crying, 'President Reagan! President Reagan!' The shots. In seconds the gunman is buried in men's bodies against a brick wall.

Next morning I said to the librarian, 'Did you hear about Ronald Reagan?'

'Yes, I did,' she said. 'I've been thinking about how clearly I remember exactly what I was doing when I heard that Kennedy had been shot. And this time I just thought, Ho hum.'

———

Dreamt I travelled a long way on a rickety train with slatted sides. I got off at a country station and saw a wonderful house that backed on to the platform: faded green corrugated iron walls, dirt floors inside, no doors; on the lower part of the roof a thick strewing of peppercorns and gum twigs; the area surrounding the house clear, uncluttered; gum trees, three or four, standing on a slight angle as in a Hans Heysen painting.

———

Australian journalist: 'Why do Americans *want* to carry guns in such large numbers?'

American politician: 'They want to carry guns because…to them…it's the symbol of life itself.'

———

Having had a child when I did has been one of the major strokes of good fortune in my life.

———

The woman calls me. Why? I hardly know her. 'I read *Honour* and I just burst into tears. It was such a relief.' She talks, through bursts of bitter laughter and occasional weeping, of her impossible marriage. I suggest timidly that she might consider leaving the whole box and dice. 'I'll never leave my children, *never*—do you understand?' she shouts. She invites me to her house for lunch. I accept out of curiosity. She is out. A maid lets me in: she *has a maid*. Soon she returns with food in white plastic bags. In her elegant clothes and high-heeled black sandals she takes awkward strides, throwing her arms around pointlessly. Chin always lifted and thrust forward in defensive posture. Her hair cut to shoulder-length, swept away to the left in a movie-star style. She's always fiddling with it but not tentatively—rather she will seize the comb that's holding it off her face, bunch the hair up at the back of her head and thrust the comb into it again, thus creating an entirely new hairdo. She did this at least ten times while I was there. Something shocking about her relationship with inanimate objects. She moved around the kitchen with violence: open a cupboard door, look inside, slam it again with a loud report. She did not seem to know where anything was. I cut up some vegetables: first I wasn't cutting fine enough, then I cut too fine, but it didn't matter, she didn't 'give a damn' how I cut them, it wasn't important to her at all. She sliced up fish and flung the whole collection of cut matter into an extremely hot wok. Trying to make conversation I mentioned a woman I did not know she hated. This drove her into a frenzy. Even trying to write this down is making me sick. We sat at the bench with our plates of food. It was delicious but I couldn't get past the brutality of its preparation. She kept jumping up to feed the cat, to push its three bowls about on a sheet of newspaper. Once she went to the back door and opened it. The autumn wind blew in and she banged it shut with a muttered word.

I call him. From the first moment I hear his voice I know that all is lost. I am once again the terrified, plain eighteen-year-old on the green telephone chair in the hall, having done the unforgivably forward thing and *rung up a boy*. The sensation is *exactly the same*. He is surprised. He draws back infinitesimally, there is a yawning gulf. Perhaps he is not even alone. I am humiliated. I hear the drawl in his voice. I am shaking with fear.

———

If it does nothing else, this whole business will turn me into a feminist again. I was about to write, 'I am terribly unhappy.' And then I thought, That is not even true.

———

After the phone call I worked on bitterly, trying to finish my review of the University of Queensland Press short story collection: the only woman in it is the naked one on the cover. I had to work very hard indeed to hold the bitterness out of my writing, while at the same time keeping criticism sharp. I think I succeeded. It's quite funny, and not particularly punishing.

———

The letter comes at long last. He plays certain notes, knows what their effect will be. I know, myself, that when I am able to write a charming letter, neither too short nor too long, striking just the right balance between literary stylishness and spontaneity, I am writing falsely, and perhaps even lying.

———

I am about to make a colossal fool of myself. I am breaking a decent man's heart. 'What can I do for you?' says F. 'Trust me,' I say, 'and leave me alone.' In case anyone should want to know, I'm crying because I was born in Australia and not in Europe, and because I'm tired and sick, and because in the taxi I read Kafka, *At Night*: 'Why are you watching? Someone must watch, it is said.

Someone must be there.'

———

My intellectual equipment has gone rusty. And has never developed to its full strength in the first place. I get frightened when I think it might be too late.

———

Yesterday M sat happily at the piano in the kitchen, playing the simplified 'Moonlight Sonata'. She had been working away at it for half an hour or so, completely absorbed, when a woman from the circus wandered in. She listened for a moment in her stoned, distracted way, then said very loudly, in a harsh voice, 'Can she play rock-and-roll as well?' 'Oh yes,' said someone hastily, 'she plays a mean boogie.' The child, oblivious, laboured on.

———

Got up at 6.30 to work. A fat, bone-coloured moon was sinking into a sky streaked pink and lavender, between the rabbit hutch and the fig tree.

———

Letters are too slow; the telephone is too fast.

———

Romantics are dangerous. They will not give up the privileges of childhood. They save up little secrets for themselves, which can become lies. Sometimes, if surprised, they turn a cold face.

———

'...Thus it is that egoists always have the last word; having laid down at the start that their determination is unshakeable, the more the sentiment in them to which one appeals to make them abandon it is touched, the more fault they find, not with themselves who resist the appeal but with those persons who put them under the necessity of resisting it, with the result that their own firmness may be carried to the utmost degree of cruelty, which only aggravates all the more in their eyes the culpability of the person who is so indelicate as to be hurt, to be in the right, and to cause them thus treacherously the pain of acting against their natural instinct of pity.' —Marcel Proust, *The Guermantes Way*

———

I feel like a bombed city. All the remaining life is underground.

———

I have to go right to the end of the story.

———

'What's attractive about you is a very charming…nastiness,' said the journalist. 'It makes you able to squeeze through cracks. Suddenly a brick is thrown, and you're gone.'

———

About writing: meaning is *in* the smallest event. It doesn't have to be *put* there: only revealed.

———

Bobby Sands died today in the Maze. There is fighting in the streets of Belfast. These things I heard on the car radio as I mastered the lane system of Sydney's streets. Will he go to hell? Is starving yourself to death counted as suicide?

———

At their table sat a wild child. A boy, androgynous (M swore he was a girl but something in his cheek-line was masculine to me) with an expressionless face, eyes slitted over high Russian cheekbones, blond hair chopped short and dyed in a skunk-like streak from brow to nape. He did not speak at all, but shovelled down a plate of soup, listening warily to the grunts and cries of what passed for conversation among the young men at his table. By the time we got to the register he was at the counter ordering a coffee. He carried it carefully to a table and drank it by lowering his face to the cup, in which still stood a spoon.

Suddenly the editor turns to me where I'm sitting behind him on a couch. 'You know what I liked, in an interview with you that I read? The way you said you write by hand. I reckon handwriting's bloody dying out.'

'Good, sensible people often withdraw from one another because of secret differences, each becoming absorbed by what he feels is right and by the error of the other. Conditions then grow more and more complicated and exasperating, until it becomes impossible to undo the knot at the crucial moment on which everything depends.'
—Goethe, *The Sorrows of Young Werther*

Small boy: 'We've got—well, him and my mum aren't married yet. A boarder. He hit her one night when he was drunk!'

    HG: 'I hope she gave him a couple of good ones back.'

    Boy: 'She was *unconscious*! She sat up and said, "What was *that* about?"'

The people next door were celebrating something with fireworks. Each of them was waving a sparkler. Their faces were soft with excitement and pleasure. M and I got hold of a cracker ('Trilogy Ground Type') and took it out to the car park to let it off. We were so busy running away, glancing back over our shoulders, that we saw only the very beginning of the explosion, and the cloud of smoke left hanging over the bare concrete. As we came back to the house, hand in hand up the lane, an answering rocket shot into the balmy air a hundred yards ahead of us, above some houses. We screeched in fright and both instinctively stepped sideways as if to press ourselves against the smooth white side wall of the house next door.

'When you're young,' said C's wife, 'you really believe that two people can make some kind of dream together; but you try it, and you get older, and you come to realise that all there is is *you*, finally.'

―――

What is the point of this diary? There is always something deeper, that I don't write, even when I think I'm saying everything.

―――

At 6 pm S came to pick me up and we ran through the park, across Heidelberg Road and the freeway, and all the way to the river, in tides of warm air and under an apricot sky. We squatted at the water's edge and watched the daylight fade and the wind stream through the gum-tree tops. A half-moon was out, high up. We walked back along the fence of the football ground. A soccer team was doing sit-ups in the dark. A parked car flicked its lights at us: a grinning, stupid face behind the windscreen.

―――

B comes home from Italy. Her boyfriend in Bologna calls her. I hear her laughing and chatting with him: '*Il cielo è molto diverso. E bellissimo.*'

―――

'It was only a joke.'
    'Jokes don't come from nowhere!'

―――

I got a cheque for $80 for a theatre review. A few months ago I was getting at least $100. Better investigate this.

―――

A piece of S's husband's childhood is for sale: thirty-five acres on a mountain out past Healesville, and on it the guesthouse, long ago closed down, that his parents used to take him to in the fifties. He drives us to see it on a windy morning. 'Out on this lawn was where they set up the cane chairs,' he says in a dreamy voice. 'The tartan rugs. The tam-o-shanters.' He is in a trance, glazed and smiling like a simpleton. We peer through the windows into tiny cabins with dark panelling and heavy furniture.

'I told her,' said F, 'it was not a matter of choice. That one's main relationship was the meal, and the other person was the condiment. If you ever had to choose, for nourishment, between a chop and some mustard, you would always choose the chop.'

I dreamt I saw myself from behind. I was wearing a top without shoulders or sleeves, and my bare back rippled with hard, glossy muscle.

B and I rode to the Fitzroy Gardens to watch the wedding parties having their photos taken. We leaned on our bikes for a long time, half hidden by vegetation, greedy for detail. Flashes of colour behind shrubbery. In the distance, great heavy elms with dark trunks, and at their base a tiny froth of white: a hurrying bride. The young Italian and Greek men wear their silly top-hats shoved to the back of the head, ears sticking out of thick hair, like louts from Eton. The Australian bride runs her day with an iron fist: her harsh, humourless voice giving orders. Australians have no sense of occasion. They stand about with shy faces that look mean. The Mediterraneans dress with unselfconscious flamboyance and play their roles with gusto.

How we fight, tooth and nail, against gaining real insight. Against letting go of what makes us suffer.

'...We know from the testimony of the Russian conspirators the incomparable feeling that overcame them in that moment of utter solitude when they reared back to throw the bomb. With the bomb they simultaneously took their own fate, that of their victim and that of their entire cause into their hand. This moment lifted them outside themselves and above everyone else...' —Hans Magnus Enzensberger, *Dreamers of the Absolute*

Derby Day at Flemington. Five hours of pure pleasure. The vast expanse of grass that made a sky-ey silence under the murmurous voices of the crowd; the women's and men's pipe bands full of children and fat-legged ladies; the horses which despite their thunder seem not to touch the ground; a strapper of ten or eleven who, leading the huge animal with its rider, has to throw his head and shoulders desperately into the neck of the horse to keep it from walking astray; the hooked, witch-like faces of the jockeys; the way the roar of the crowd travels along parallel with the horses until it reaches you and swallows you up and you're helping to make it. Two old ladies stood beside us, laughing like schoolgirls at the fashionable people inside their wire enclosure, the merciless women with hard, thin lips and ambitious eyes. 'There's two or three centuries in there,' said B. 'There are *no reference points*.' 'Look at that white dress!' said one of the old ladies. 'Those dangly bits are like albs. What bishops wear.' 'And her head-dress is like what Arabs wear,' I said. We all doubled up, hanging on to the green railing, keeping our hands carefully between the very sharp green spikes.

In fifteen minutes I'll be thirty-nine years old.

In any interlocking group of three, information flows in and out, like tides, and at any given moment no one person is in possession of a fair share of it.

The kitchen in the house we've rented: as soon as I walked through the back door I knew that someone had been happy in it. Something to do with yellow light, or cream walls, or a plenteous sense of organisation. At my old ladies' writing class we chanced to talk about this instinctive certainty. Every one of them agreed vehemently that it was a power of reception found almost exclusively in women. 'We had a fight about a house once,' said one of them. 'My husband was looking at timber and windows and measurements, but I said *no*. I couldn't live here. He was furious.'

———

A sign on the wall at the Learning Exchange: a bloke is seeking someone who'd like to 'engage in non-competitive fencing bouts'.

———

Walking the dog in the old, forgotten parts of the cemetery. Milk thistles stand as high as your shoulder, dry grasses bend in the wind between the slabs of grey stone. In pockets, among the Emma Elizas and Charles Edwards, lie Panagiotis, Ahmed, Julio. Huge sky. Rain threatening.

———

'Can I come in here and hang around you? I just want to be near you.'

———

On community radio, the young announcer's voice was deep with outrage: 'For those listeners who wondered why, instead of last week's anti-uranium show, there was half an hour of the Beach Boys, it was because *somebody* "mislaid the tape"—what's that phone ringing? They're trying to stop this one too.' *Oooh*. A conspiracy. Still, we went to the demo. It was quite big. A man near us said he wished there were more 'ordinary-looking people from the suburbs. Remember the Moratorium marches?' B says demos are a waste of time, and that she is thinking of joining a party. She was talking about the ALP. Surely that would complete her disillusionment?

———

The old historian rang. We met at a weird place in Swanston Street called Cafe Nostalgia, furnished with old dining-room tables of the massive, polished kind. He is a gossip. Mostly I listen. He'll never get it, about women. When I ironically used the expression 'according to the orthodoxy of the women's liberation movement', he jumped in his seat as if he'd been shot.

———

I was invited to a 'come as your heroine' party. I wore cream clothes and a surgeon's mask: Sister Vivian Bullwinkel. No one but the oldest woman present recognised the name. She herself was dressed as Boadicea. I looked up Boadicea later in the encyclopedia and was astonished to learn of her exploits.

———

A man is being tried for allegedly stabbing to death a five-year-old boy in a school dunny. The child and his eleven-year-old companion had been sent to the corner shop. On their way home they threw a stone at the accused, who took them into the dunny, 'indecently assaulted' one or both of them, then said he would have to kill them because they would tell on him to the police. The eleven-year-old escaped when the murderer heard voices approaching and hopped up to look over the wall. Later the five-year-old's body was found, full of stab wounds. The eleven-year-old said in court that the dead boy had offered the man a dollar to spare his life.

———

Jessye Norman at the Town Hall. Big as a haystack, with a small, dramatic head, tiny hands and immense, slow, graceful gestures. She strolled, like the mountain coming to Mahomet, from the wings to her work position beside the Steinway, at which crouched the wizened, bent-backed Félix Lavilla, and then stood quite still for a good three minutes, gaze lowered to her clasped hands, composing herself after that exertion. Her voice I cannot describe. She ended each song with mouth wide open, an expression of ecstatic delight, eyes up-turned to the balcony.

I can't bear it when people I know haven't *become happier.*

My short story was rejected by the *Bulletin* because it contained four-letter words. A letter from Geoffrey Dutton: 'It pains me to have to knock this back…It's you at your best.' Thanks a lot. I suppose he's a skilled writer of rejection letters.

Mansfield Park. She never tells you anything about the appearance of her characters. As if they were moral forces. I love it.

Another friendship murdered in the name of sexual freedom and sexual fidelity. Jammed in the middle and squashed till blood came out of its eyes and ears.

On TV I saw the Pope touching people and speaking to them. He was wearing a little silk cap. He moved along a row of people, stretching out his hands in a quiet, formal manner, smiling and nodding, leaning to them. Someone held up a child and out came his hand, fingers spread star-wise, like a blind man's, to touch the child's cheeks and temple. His movements were so extremely slow (as if the film were being run at half speed, though the movements of people around him were normal) that I wondered if this were not the source of the extraordinary power of the little scene, although it was on the screen only a few seconds.

The young woman talks relentlessly, her pretty, broad-mouthed face lit with intelligence, her permed brown hair quivering. So eager to impress.

1982

Two young girls write a story and run outside, leaving the page on the table: 'Sorrow, destruction, riots, death, starvation, wars, depression, unhappiness, poverty, black market, slaves, civil wars, battles, ghetto's, racism, predudice, bigots, suffering, crime, generation gaps, sadness, hopelessness and 10 000 000 other tradgedies would evolve when he was gone.'

―――

S rang to say her husband was ill and in pain: she took him to the doctor who found a little lump in his groin and sent him straight to the Alfred. 'He dropped his bundle,' she said. 'He was all cold and white and shivering.' She went to Dimmey's and bought him a pair of cotton pyjamas, fawn with a maroon pattern.

―――

I dreamt that the Russians surprised everyone by invading Czechoslovakia again.

―――

B and I tried to do the *National Times* 'Great Literary Quiz' and got about one in ten. So what, I say, ashamed. She's always told me she doesn't know anything about poetry but I never believed her till she failed to recognise *'There was movement at the station…'*

―――

Circus Oz is loading itself into its prepared vans, trucks and caravans, ready to depart for good from the Pram Factory tomorrow, they say. I hang around upstairs in the Tower watching people busily come and go. One of the oldest performers stops to speak to me. She seems cheerful but suddenly turns her face away and covers it with one hand. Past her bowed shoulders I see that huge chest-high weeds have forced their way unchallenged between the terra cotta tiles of the patio at the end of the hallway.

———

Apparently I am bossy, impatient, ill-mannered and a hypocrite. I also don't like the way I look, much. It's probably mostly the haircut. The waiters at l'Aquila obviously think B and I are lesbians.

———

The hottest night that's ever been recorded: still 32 degrees at 6 am. I lay all night with my feet pointed towards the window through which poured a stream of anti-human wind, hot and dry, straight off a desert. A glaring moon. The only way to fall asleep was to have a cool shower and lie, still wet, on a towel with a damp nightie spread over me. But as soon as the water evaporated I woke.

———

I am teaching myself to embroider. I stitched three little fish on the edge of a pillowcase. 'The iron and the damp cloth,' says the neighbour. 'Everything will become smooth and flat.'

———

Sometimes ideas for stories surface as if from a muddy pond. I'd like to write about a young savage. I would need an older sister character, rather shadowy. Could the elder sister and another woman be in conflict for the savage's…what? Allegiance? Certainly not mind. Possession. I don't know.

———

In the cafe we were talking about coprophagy. A woman went to say 'fetish' but stopped at 'fet—', realising it was the wrong term. One of the men saw the moment of hesitation and went in boots first. 'I know it's not the right word!' she yelled. 'I was trying to think of the correct one! Can't anyone make a mistake?' 'It's as if you called a chair a table!' he shouted, seizing a chair, banging the flat of his hand on the table.

At the music school I felt like bawling with envy as I walked along a wet path between two buildings in which children practised in small rooms: oboes, strings. The way M bows with her skinny brown arm, jumps her fingers up and down the strings. Her eyes stare at the music without blinking, like a surgeon's when he operates, cuts flesh.

Now I'm making a living from freelance journalism I keep having an irritable feeling that newspapers are hysterical and silly; that the rush to fill their pages, especially the magazine sections in which stuff like mine is published, is bad for people, bad for the newspaper, bad for *me*.

I asked my sister to show me her caesarean scar. It was less drastic than I'd imagined: horizontal, slightly curved upwards like a faint smile, neatly cut near a natural wrinkle in the skin of her belly. It was healing beautifully. Really it's a wonder that people ever die. The other day I read about Vivian Bullwinkel and the bullet that the Japanese shot into her at the massacre of Banka Island: it went straight through her from back to front, and missed her vital organs—and the wound never became infected, though they were in the tropics. She put this down to the length of time she spent in salt water, in the hours and days after the massacre.

I heard third-hand from New York that a 'very famous old woman writer' had read *Honour* and wanted me to come to Columbia for a term to teach in her course. My informant had left at home the piece of paper with the old writer's name on it. It turned out to be Grace Paley. Surely this can't possibly be true. I called my sister and told her about it. 'Wow!' she said. 'But I hate her stuff.'

———

The chiropractor had gone quite grey since the last time I saw him. His hands were shockingly strong. He put me on my back and pulled my head towards him: a crack, and a distinct ripple right down my spine, as of beads on a string jerked out straight. 'Ah, lovely,' he said to himself.

———

G told me about a place he went to in London called the Comedy Store. 'There was this line-up of comics, breaking their necks to get to the mike. One would get booed, the gong would go and he'd get hustled off—another would be pushing forward to take his place. The audience was full of people with really developed consciousness. Any hint of sexism and he wouldn't just get abuse—there'd be a torrent of hamburgers, and rubbish. It was as if the audience was dragging the comics up to its level.'

———

Today I saw a US review of *Honour*. 'Drably clinical', 'hang-loose, dreary, quasi-commune living', 'with some mirthless humour', 'lacking in narrative shape and occasionally over-written'…; however, 'these vignettes of disordered domestic life are fleetingly affecting…all in all, promising glimpses—more so than in *Monkey Grip*—of a limited but tangible talent.' It's probably true that my 'talent' is limited. My range is, anyway. Or so I am always being told.

———

As dark fell, a faint light glimmered on the undersides of the eucalypt branches. It slithered between their narrow leaves, making them strongly three-dimensional. A young man remarked to me, as I stood sober in the middle of the garden, 'Have to get 'em dancing soon, over there on the grass. They're too bloody arrogant to dance unless we make 'em.' 'Oh, they're probably just shy.' '*Shy?*' He turned his head away in irritation, then whirled back: 'Shyness and arrogance are two sides of the same coin.'

'He panicked,' she said. 'It was like going out with a trainee priest.'

Our friend is only part way through the surgery, but one is already to use the word *she*. This is not difficult. Late in the afternoon we all drove to Bronte and swam in the surf. A light mist of spray hung over the water. The sand was extraordinarily clean and pale. She wore pink bathers with bra cups and a little skirt. She has narrow hips and long thighs like a man, but a woman's skin: white, smooth, and rather tender. When we came home she left her hair messy and it dried curly. She tied a bright red scarf round her head in a band, and black curls escaped over her neck and forehead so prettily that I kept glancing at her. Her beauty was touching, somehow; the result of drastic decisions, yet vivid and spontaneous. We got talking about modes of greeting in different languages and cultures. 'I like it in France,' I said, 'the way when you go into a shop they just say "*m'sieu*" or "*madame*"—they greet you according to your sex.' At this she pulled a face of comic dismay so exaggerated that we all burst out laughing.

First old lady in writing class: 'What does everyone do on Sunday mornings?'

Second old lady, like a shot, with a smug smile: '*I* go to church. What do *you* do?'

'Probably writes in her diary,' I refrained from saying, 'which is witty, unlike the "poetry" and "natural description" that *you* turn out.'

———

I don't know much about getting on with people. I'm as selfish as a cat. I don't like cats and I never have. I would like to write about dominance, revulsion, separation, the horrible struggles between people who love each other.

———

The play veered between being really funny and wallowing in embarrassing sentimentality. 'There's nothing wrong with sentiment, as long as it's not masquerading as real feeling,' said Professor Maxwell at Melbourne University twenty years ago. But in this case it *is* masquerading. Sentimentality keeps looking over its shoulder to see how you're taking it. Emotion doesn't give a shit whether anyone's looking or not.

———

The young savage is wearing a very small, bright blue bikini made of three ruched hearts. She bounds up the concrete steps to kiss me. 'It's my birthday! I'm twenty-two and I'm *so drunk*!' We watch her skip away and plunge into the pool. The mother next to me lets out her breath: 'It hasn't even got a strap to hold it up.'

———

The naturopath said my blood pressure was low. This surprised me. I always imagine it's so high that the top of my head is about to blow off.

———

My sister comes to stay while she does a training course at a big hospital. I have the annoyance of new Levis. Stiff, biting at the waist. 'I look awful in these jeans. All out of shape.' 'Listen,' she says, 'I'll take you out to the Austin and show you some *really* misshapen bodies.'

M went to a farm and had her feet stepped on by two horses. One at a time.

'I therefore advise young people to adopt the practice of beautiful women and *to care for their line*, to prefer the lean to the fat. And not to look at themselves in a mirror, but simply to look at themselves.'
—Jean Cocteau, *On Line*

Girl: 'Why do you have to go to Adelaide for ten days?'
　　Mother: 'It's a writers' festival. It's work.'
　　Girl: 'But I can't live without you.'
　　Mother: 'Oh, you can so.'
　　Girl: 'Well of course I *can*. But I hate it.'
　　Mother: 'Why don't you like it?'
　　Girl: 'I like it when you get up in the morning and I like it when you're there when I get home from school. And no one will kiss me goodnight.'
　　Mother: 'Somebody else could.'
　　Girl: 'Yes, but it's not the same.'

As I approached the back gate I could hear The Police, very loud. I expected to see M and her friend dancing, but when I got to the kitchen door I saw two neat little lassies sitting opposite each other at the table, doing their homework.

In the bus full of writers, an Englishman takes the seat beside me: 'Do you mind my talking to you?'
　　'Course not. What'll we talk about?' 'Shall we get right down to it and talk about sex?' We laugh. 'Why don't you describe your wife?' 'Okay. She's got a naughty face. Now, your husband.' 'He's

got a big round head and he's very funny.' Behind us is sitting a quiet New Zealander, a Maori. The Englishman invites her into our game: 'What does your house look like?' 'Well, it's made of asbestos. It's behind my brother's house, so we had to build up higher to get a view over his place to the sea.' 'What are your ambitions?' asks the Englishman, 'and don't ask me mine, 'cause I don't know.' 'I want to live a long time,' says the Maori woman, 'because I've got a lot of things I want to write.' I say, 'I want to stay married.' I start to feel carsick from turning around in my seat.

———

At the mighty fireworks display a little girl sobbed desperately, clinging to her father's leg, while her younger brother gaped upwards, silent with wonder, one fist firmly attached to his father's trousers. An Italian man standing near us, distressed by her panicky weeping, murmured furtively to the little girl: 'Are you scared?' 'What do you want me to *do*?' said the father to the girl, bemused and cross. Pick her up, you moron.

———

The English writer believes in turning the other cheek. 'A magazine I knew was going out of business published a harsh attack on me, so I sent them a cheque for twenty-five quid. In the following issue they ran an even worse one, so I sent them a second cheque for the same amount. After that, it stopped.'

———

The way people with terrible hangovers feel obliged to think up an entrance line at breakfast. 'Anyone get the number of that truck that hit us?' 'Kindly explain why you punched me last night.'

———

HG: 'What's it like when your children grow up and move out?'
    Japanese writer: 'Merit is greater than sadness.'

———

The academic talked to me about teaching: 'I realised I was wasting a lot of time making sure that all the students *liked* me.'

Ka-blam. So that's why I'm always exhausted after a class.

'Charming people is very tiring, isn't it,' I said.

'Not only charming them, but constantly checking to see if it's working.'

———

I stick my head out the window and bang! A fat sun, gold as gold, hits me full in the face. I walk down the stairs into a well of yellow. The sun is bursting through any crack it can find. The air itself is shining. I come upstairs again, carrying two cups of coffee and the hem of my nightie. The closed door of F's room is a rectangle of wood barely holding back the eastern light. It is rimmed in gold, and through the keyhole shoots a narrow bolt of sun.

———

With a pair of short-bladed scissors the Chinese street-artist cut out a rooster from a small piece of paper. The only hint of expression in his face as he worked was a slight knotting or bulging of the flesh between his eyebrows; this was also his only mark of ageing. He seemed to keep the scissors still, and to move the paper.

———

When we walk down the street I notice G's eyes following a certain kind of woman. It's a game with me to '*suivre son regard*', to pick which ones he'll like the look of. I usually get it right. I enjoy watching his senses register. I don't know if he knows I'm doing it and I don't care. He's making a mess of his life. I don't think I'm much good to him as a friend. Maybe he likes to be with me because he can talk about writing, which seems to be the rock he's standing on in the rising flood.

———

The harpsichordist was wearing a very attractive dress with a belt and a collar and a lot of skirt, and long sleeves which she had unbuttoned at the wrist and rolled up to the elbow. Her thick, frizzy hair was pulled into a knob on top of her head. She had a perfect pink and white complexion. After the first piece she took a tissue out of her sleeve and blew her nose, which turned a darker pink and then faded.

———

B and I went to see *As You Like It* at the Melbourne Theatre Company. We laughed so much in the first half that tears ran down our cheeks. There were two empty seats in the front row so at interval we went down and sat in them. A man behind us: '*Tsk*. I can't *bear* it when people take seats they've got no right to.' His female companion: 'Do you want to move?' 'I certainly *do*.' Tomorrow I have to write my review. Wish I could write about the snotty couple and leave the play alone.

———

Indian summer. Mild air from the north, dust rises, skies at night are velvet. In the park the ground is hard: cracks have appeared, whiskers of grass tinge dry earth with green where yesterday, perhaps, a hose sprinkled.

———

F gets four days off work and becomes very cheerful and entertaining. His teeth flash at the table. He walks around the house singing a phrase or two like Teresa Stratas: falsetto, quite pure and clear, and true.

———

Something in the snubbed shape of the woman's nose makes me suspect trouble—or maybe it's the stuff she comes out with. She declares that a menstruating woman can prevent plants from growing merely by walking through a garden. 'What is the reason?' I ask. 'Well, I know that just before my period my energy field is in such a mess that it could easily affect another one nearby.' When I approach the table carrying three apples and a knife she cries out: 'You're not going to *peel* them, are you?' She is trying to finish her university degree: she says she's always stopped before, 'to go and look at clouds for a while', or 'because the pressure on me was too much'.

Everyone at the table longs to pull the whining, manipulative child into line. His mother is at his mercy. 'I've heard,' she says helplessly, 'that it's safe to hit them just here, on the side of the thigh.' F remarks that his parents used to hit him across the face. His father's blow would leave a hand-shaped mark with a red ridge around it.

New director of the museum: 'Like to come and see our Fred Williamses?'

HG: (*nervously*) 'Yes please.'

Director: (*striding through the glass and china section*) 'Got to change all this.'

HG: 'Why? I quite like it.'

Director: 'Too samely. Too bland. We'll rip out all this and make—you know, the silver all together in one place—darker—so people get that secret feeling that they've found the treasure themselves.'

We arrive at the Fred Williams paintings. I stand in front of them blind with nerves and ignorance. Away he goes, telling and showing in his red-and-white striped shirt and red velvet bow tie and black suit. As I look and listen, the responsibility for speech having been deftly removed from me, I begin to see the things he speaks about: warm or cold surfaces, smooth or roughened; lumps of paint, the suggestion of a grid; 'the essence of the country—repetitive marks on a huge emptiness—but fleeting, fleeting'. I'm breathless, dizzy:

being offered the gift of sight. I would have followed him all over the gallery. In front of one painting, having made a few remarks, he says, 'Do you like it?' 'Oh yes! It's *beautiful*!'

———

G's daughter pulls an office chair up to the piano and sprinkles her fingers over the keyboard. Her father speaks to her in the middle of the piece, which she is rendering in a slummocky manner. She looks up at him and answers, swivels the chair towards him, but continues to play, as if her mind and her hands had nothing to do with each other.

———

'Oh, Helen!' says M. 'I'm in love with Tom Burlinson!'
   'Who?'
   'You know! In *The Man from Snowy River*! Dee and I played all day, pretending we were in a movie and at the end we were having a party for the cast and crew. We had this disconnected old black phone, and rang up all the famous people we knew and invited them. And when we finished the game we felt really awful.'

———

My scary auntie tells me about seeing a ninety-year-old woman neglected by the staff in a nursing home: 'Stupid goats—they didn't see she was euchred. A bit light-on. Not the full bob. She had that gurgling business you get with pneumonia.'

———

'Wanna hear something terrific?' I squatted beside the stereo and put on a track of Sviatoslav Richter playing *The Well-Tempered Clavier*. G stood in the middle of the room. As the music ran, bounced and thickened he gave a few little grunts of pleasure, then threw back his head and laughed out loud.

———

'We don't really know it, but we sense it: there is a sister ship to our life which takes a totally different route. While the sun burns behind the islands.' —Tomas Tranströmer in *The Blue House*

How it's done. 'At that party I had,' said G, 'the big new Carlton dealer came sidling up and slipped me a little bit of heroin. I laughed and put it into a cigarette and smoked it. Later he slid up to me again and said he had a lot of it to unload and did I want to buy some. I said I had no money. But he sort of nodded round the room and said, "Look—there's at least five people here who use—why don't you just do a whip-around? You'll get the price of a deal." I said I didn't want to.' G spoke with a kind of disgust, putting it on for my benefit.

I was practising the piano, rather sloppily I suppose, while F washed the dishes. He came in when I'd finished and said, 'I think what you should do is play the piano when I'm not here. It's pretty annoying.'

Two buses crash in France and forty-four children die. One report says the drivers were racing, flicking their lights on and off, and hit a broken-down car with no lights. Everything and everyone burned except one boy, who was later found wandering nearby, shocked out of his mind. On TV, forty-four coffins made of pale, polished timber are lined up in what looks like a school gymnasium. Outside, banks of flowers. On one coffin—and surely many more—a hand-lettered card: ENFANT NON-IDENTIFIÉ. A cavalcade of square, glass-sided hearses winds up a hilly road with houses on one side and a high brick wall on the other.

We found a place to park the Kombi—up behind Lorne where the ground fell away on all sides and huge, pale-trunked gums, with strips of bark lying about their feet, soared up into a night sky absolutely milky with stars. We lit a fire. Wind rushed through the tops of the trees, and sometimes rushed also on ground level: I had to hold down the lighter bits of my fire with a stick. Odd sounds. I was scared. A bird whipping a hundred metres away in the dark.

———

When the woman speaks at length she slides her eyes away to the left and rattles out her clever, well-expressed thoughts with a constant smile, as if amused by something she sees over your shoulder. And she grimaces and distorts her features while she thinks and talks, trying perhaps to distract attention from the un-beauty of her face by keeping it in motion.

———

At the pub B wrote herself off. She was too drunk to take her contact lenses out—she passed out, mumbling, 'All I want is to be *warm*.' So I put her into her bed and covered her up, and hoped the lenses wouldn't bore their way into her eyes during the night.

———

G said he learnt how to stand, at parties and clubs, from black men he saw in London: 'back to the wall *but not leaning*; head up, eyes narrowed.'

———

Virginia Woolf, in her diary, often writes that she's not up to the job of recording her encounters with her friends, but she launches on it anyway and is soon merrily swimming along. Very sharp, especially about other women.

———

On the other side of the river is New South Wales. I wish this fact had greater significance, or that I could write, 'On the other side of this river is Spain, or the Sudan. Or Brazil.' Always wishing for romance, ho hum, and anyway I can't speak Spanish. Or Portuguese.

———

In *The Aunt's Story* he says, about Theodora, that she is not creative, that she has not got 'the artist's vanity'.

———

Waxworks, in Echuca. I'd never seen one before. B and I got the giggles, being the only people there. We noticed that the most obvious failures were two modern characters, John and Robert Kennedy. In their suits, with their anxious, businessmen's faces, they could have been anybody. Nasser and King Hussein were terrific. Funny how they can't get the feet to look real. They should get worn-out shoes and polish them, instead of using stiff, new ones.

———

The biographer came for a cup of tea and played some Bach on our piano. She coaxed me to play and I did, and when I got lost she was just *friendly*. She said, 'I love Bach's resolutions', and simple things that seemed important to say. I told her I'd been asked not to play when anyone else is home. She laughed, but she was shocked.

———

I could develop a real passion for Graham Greene: 'Even at night the air was so humid that it broke upon the cheek like tiny beads of rain.'

———

This is my fifth day without coffee, tea or alcohol. I have still got iron bars in my shoulders, but I am not full of mad haste to nowhere. I notice that a glass of water is sufficient, in conversation, for something to raise occasionally to my mouth.

———

At the Last Laugh I met a boy called Noah Taylor. His face was smooth, round-cheeked, absolutely unmarked, solemn, thoughtful, weird. A round forehead, above which rose a peculiar black beret.

———

I really like reviewing plays. What I love about it is the necessity to think back to, and formalise, what I really felt or thought in the theatre.

In the Kombi on the way home M used the word *pedantic* in its correct and appropriate sense. 'Where'd you pick that up?' 'At school. Miss Saunders taught it to us.' 'It's got a rather negative connotation, hasn't it.' 'What's that mean?' 'Well, it's never a compliment.' 'I see. Maybe I should try to use it in the exam, if it fits.' Days later she reports that she got it into her essay at the MacRob entrance exam.

The horrible saga of a breaking marriage. The child tells his father, innocently, that the other man has been in the house. The father goes berserk: 'It's territorial. He's been in my *house*.' I am drawn to the drama. At first I thought he had it coming to him. Now I see how he's suffering. And she reminds me of myself. Behaving with a queenly, detached selfishness that shocks and enrages people. 'Matilda told such dreadful lies,/ It made one gasp and stretch one's eyes.' Well—I was never much of a liar. I tended rather to tell the truth and expect people to cop it.

I rode my bike to my piano lesson. I'm not so afraid of making a fool of myself now. As I merrily tinkled away, saying 'Oh shit' whenever I made a mistake, she said, 'I think you should do an exam. You'd be sure to get an A. You're very, very musical. You notice things in the music that others don't see.' Bathed in joy, I nonetheless thought, Tell that to the people I live with.

I make up my bed every night as deliciously as if for a sick person I was looking after.

Man behind the counter in the post office, to his colleague: 'It took her quite a while to calm down, after I slapped her face, Frank. Yes, I've always told her that if there's one thing I won't allow it's telling me what to do when I'm driving. I just reached across and hit her. Because we were passing the spot where a few years ago I was nearly involved in a very serious accident.'

―――

A girl waiting for the lights in Bourke Street last Tuesday. A perfect example of how I would like to look: not her face, but her way of dressing: practical, comfortable, colourful, not fashionable. Straight black skirt just below the knees, a mauve-ish jumper, red stockings, brown flat shoes, green gloves, and a little red knapsack on her back. She looked *terrific*. M teased me for turning back, again and again, open-mouthed, to stare after her.

―――

A reviewer of a collection of women's diaries from the late eighteenth century is surprised to find that they're about family affairs and do not mention the French Revolution. I don't find this at all surprising. But now that I'm sitting up in bed, pen in hand, on a rainy Saturday afternoon, all my little stored-up treasures turn their backs and hide in the shrubbery.

―――

The man at the meeting had a tense and rather sexual presence. I mean, he couldn't seem to look at a woman in an ordinary way. A challenging sexuality was behind his eyes. A slightly pugnacious way of tilting his head back to look at you.

―――

In the magazine the subs once again make me look an idiot. All my jokes cut out, the tone violated, the central argument truncated. I cry over it. I feel like resigning. I've felt like this a hundred times before and haven't done it. Oh, if only I knew I had a grant I'd tell the *National Times* to cram it.

———

M and her teacher play a little duet on their cellos. Sight-reading. How the hell do they do it? The note on the page, move fingers to prepare strings, keep the bow moving—up or down as indicated—no wonder musicians' eyes are so staring and fixed. 'Look at ya thumb!' cries the teacher. 'Ya thumb's like a crippled crab crawling!' They tackle a piece called *'L'Orientale'*. He shouts at her: 'You sound as if some Arab had stabbed you and you'd fallen across the strings!'

———

The boy is skinny, with a pale, fine-boned, waxy-skinned face, a kind of manic energy, a loud, shrill voice, obsessive behaviour. He loves matches and fire.

———

Why I like the English language: because it contains words like *cup*. Fat, short and stumpy, and rather optimistic.

———

I got a one-year grant. I rented a room in the Nicholas Building. Ninety dollars a month. It faces north. A fair amount of sky hangs outside its windows. Faintly, from the City Square nine floors below, a brass band. I will get curtains. I will get a weekly tram card. I will be a working woman.

———

I'm supposed to be interviewing the composer. But I'd rather just sit and watch the way he unobtrusively smokes a little rounded wooden pipe with a curved stem and a fine silver joint. Between puffs he cradles it in his half-closed hand, which rests palm-up on his long thigh. Later I type up my notes and find them curiously flat. All the magic I thought was in what he said must have come from something other than his words—his manner of speaking, his very calm solid presence. I don't *think* I invented him.

I feel like sending the writer who got a harsh review a letter of encouragement. But I haven't read his books and I probably never will.

———

I turn forty. M gives me a pack of cards and an American book of rules for card-games written in clear and simple prose. We're sitting on my bed at seven in the morning, slowly and carefully teaching ourselves draw poker, when F comes to join in and does what my father would have done: gets himself dealt into the game, grasps the rules at once, and then with a challenging grin refuses to abide by them. It's a birthday, we don't want to fight. So we do what women do: we fade away. We put down the cards quietly and go about our business.

———

I lay on my bed and read the *Paris Review* interviews. I kept dozing off. Nabokov: too clever and nasty. Kerouac: vain and noisy, a show-off. Eudora Welty: a nice, dear old lady full of respect and modesty.

———

HG: 'What are you working on?'

Sydney writer: 'I'm doing a dramatisation of the Azaria Chamberlain case. It has all the elements of Greek tragedy.'

HG: 'What are they?'

SW: 'Oh...rural setting. Baby. Sacrifice...'

HG: '...Intervention by an animal...'

SW: '...Religion...the pitting of man against circumstance or...'

HG: '...Fate...'

SW: 'A chorus.'

HG: 'Who's the chorus?'

SW: 'The press.'

HG: 'Oh, yes! How did you find out about Greek tragedy? Did you already know a lot about it?'

SW: 'No. I looked it up.'

HG: 'Do you mean you read some?'

SW: 'No. I looked it up in the *Oxford Companion to Ancient Literature*, and they had it all set out.'

At three in the morning the wind got up and blew everything about in my room but it smelled so sweet of the coming rain that I couldn't shut the window. I just bunched up the curtain and thrust it through the gap and now it's damp.

'No one was allowed to leave the theatre during his recitals, however pressing the reason. We read of women in the audience giving birth, and of men being so bored with listening and applauding that they furtively dropped down from the wall at the rear, since the gates were kept barred, or shammed dead and were carried away for burial... To destroy every trace of previous winners in these contests he ordered all their statues and busts to be taken down, dragged away with hooks, and hurled into public lavatories.' —Suetonius, about Nero, in *The Twelve Caesars*

On TV I saw the Queen Mother leaving a hospital. She had been rushed there to have a fishbone removed from her throat. As she emerged to her limousine, dressed in sky blue with one of those terrible turned-back hats in the same colour, cries arose from people in the small crowd that had gathered: 'How are you feeling? How are you *feeling*?'

A letter comes from the West Australian writer. What an unusual character he is! Four pages numbered in the Roman style, full of encouragement, embarrassment for presumption, reports on his progress. I feast on it, an intelligent and enthusiastic mind all optimistic.

———

At the meeting a new person entered, one of those balding men in their fifties with alert eyes that fix the women present in an eager stare. I felt riveted by him and had to drop my gaze. To hide this response I kept glancing at a vulgar chain bracelet of heavy silver that he wore on his left wrist. I can't take seriously a man who would wear such a thing. And yet I noticed him, and he knew that I did, and this made me furious.

———

The little boy's mouth is so stiff that he can hardly speak. When I greeted him he pointed his lips in and out, like a fish. Poor little fellow. He is wretched and whiny and hard to love. Even within his hearing she can't stop talking about her controlling husband, telling and retelling the story of their escape from him. The child stands there listening with a white face, hands at his sides like a ghostly little soldier.

———

F offered to pay some of my expenses so I could stop doing journalism and concentrate on my own work. I felt a stab of panic at the thought of being dependent.

1983

'They asked me if I went out much,' B reports. 'I said no, that I'd like to go out dancing more often but I had no one to go with. And *then* they asked me why I didn't go to places like Inflation! *Inflation*! It's only one step up from a singles' bar.'

―――

M comes back from the toilet at Notturno and tells me she's seen some graffiti of mine in there. 'What did it say?' 'I don't remember, but I recognised your writing.' I go out there to check. Someone has written, 'What happened to the graffiti? Nobody writes it any more.' Underneath it, in my neat teacher's printing: 'It was fun for a while, but it got too personal.'

―――

Two new teachers at the gym. Country-and-western women with mountains of teased bleached hair. One was wearing a leotard with a fringe up one arm, across the body and down the other leg. She looked like a kid who lies down in the shallow surf and stands up with a long strand of seaweed draped over one shoulder.

―――

'I met a woman who says she lives in the room where *Monkey Grip* was written.'

   'Bullshit. I wrote it in the State Library.'

The beginner will cling and cling to her thin first draft. She clings to the coast and will strike out into the ocean only under extreme duress.

———

At the Carlton baths, mothers as massive as sea lions lie about in groups with numerous kids under ten, at whom they squall and grunt. Also present are girls in their late teens, several of whom are pregnant. They eat hot chips out of white paper, and drink can after can of Tab. They don't have much of a handle on language. In fact they seem almost brain-damaged.

———

Flickers of a dream I once had are flashing in the corners, today. About a building, that's all I can get hold of. Must be just chemicals shunting around up there.

———

She went off to MacRob for the first time this morning, looking like a pretty insect in the uniform, her skinny brown legs ending in enormous new black shoes. 'Perhaps I'll get a nickname for having big feet!' she said with an excited laugh. 'From my *friends*!'

———

D. H. Lawrence uses the same word over and over till he makes it mean what he needs it to.

———

At Tamani I ran into a guy I used to know. He was with a friend. He told me he was getting married.
    HG: 'Oh, good! Who to?'
    Him: 'To a girl called—' (*goes blank*)
    HG: (*shocked laugh*)
    Friend: 'Stella.'
    Him: 'Oh, yes. Stella.'

HG: 'How did you meet?'

Him: 'I met her at a party. She took me home to bed, and the next morning she said, "Let's get married."'

———

I went with G to the post office so he could send some cocaine in an envelope marked WIZO—Women's International Zionist Organisation—to his friend in Sydney. The jolly lady behind the counter felt the envelope and tried to pass it through the testing slot. It wouldn't go: it would cost forty cents instead of twenty-seven. At this point I did not know what was in the envelope, although, while the friendly woman palpated it, I was beginning to guess. I concealed my dismay. G was absolutely relaxed. He smiled at her and said, 'Too thick, is it? Oh, I'll just pay the extra.'

———

Riding home, I passed the flats just as a car parked inside the fence caught fire. Thick flames wriggled out of its windows, and smoke rolled away to the north-east through the traffic on Princes Street. A young girl with a plait down her back was in a phone box barely six feet away from the burning car. The branches of an overhanging tree began to crackle and snap, right above the box, but she calmly finished her call, opened the door and walked away without a glance. The car was gushing flame. Its back windows were closed but they melted and flames flowed out through them, and through the windscreen. A wild-looking man with a carton of beer in his arms stopped near me to watch. We exchanged awed looks. 'I don't want to sound cynical,' he said, 'but my guess is that somebody lit it on purpose.'

———

Tears came to B's eyes. Suddenly her face lost its guarded, ironic look and became beautiful. I had forgotten that her eyes were such a vivid blue.

The Jungian says that dreams are messages to the conscious mind from the unconscious, which has picked up a vibe that the conscious mind is unable to perceive. He also says, I think, that the people we dream of often represent aspects of ourselves we would prefer to ignore or suppress. I wonder if it's possible to analyse one's dreams in any useful way.

At 8.30 pm I took the dog for a walk. The temperature was 42 degrees and it was dark because of a thick layer of dust in the air. I was halfway down McPherson Street when a great wind swung around behind me, coming from the south-west. The temperature dropped ten degrees in seconds. Dust flew. I had to cover my eyes. The air stank of burning and was full of smoke, the small trees whipped about. I kept walking, excited and scared. Down a lane behind a car a huge sheet of paper rose vertical into the air and danced there. People ran to their gates. 'Where's the fire?' 'Outside the city.' In another house the front window was closed tight but the curtains were open. I saw a table set formally for a dinner party, white cloth and red candles, and a beautiful young woman with thick black hair, wearing a red dress, standing at the table talking to her husband who was only a shoulder in a brown suit, half out of the room.

B describes Luciano Pavarotti's mouth, when he sings, as 'pastie-shaped'. He doesn't move his lips to shape the sound. It's all controlled elsewhere.

I've started to write, without thought of form: it keeps coming, I am happy and no longer straining after effect. But each morning I set out for my office weak with fear. I will never be a great writer. The best I can do is to write books that are small but oblique enough to stick in people's gullets so that they remember them.

———

The mountains were almost hidden in cloud. The sun rose between two dunes, huge and orange, I couldn't look at it, it was so bright. I felt like prostrating myself.

———

The woman at the next table appeared to have been crying for hours: there was something odd about her eyes under the wavy fringe. The man, who had an RAF moustache, talked a lot, with a smile, insisting gently on her attention. She asked him to buy her some matches, and he jumped to his feet. I thought they were a couple breaking up, but one of the others suggested she might have lost someone in the bushfires.

———

F came after work to inspect the house I had found. It was a terrifically hot day. He walked very slowly from room to room. The estate agent, a tactful old man, sat on a chair and took off one of his shoes. I suppose he guessed he would not be making a sale.

———

I spent only three-quarters of an hour at my office, because of agitation, too much coffee, lateness, distractions and so on, but I felt it was time well spent, for I can see 'dimly-lit pathways' into the forest of a book. I've got Alexander, Athena, Philip. They are established and already their names belong to them. Now I must take charge of them, lead them away from the literal past, start to snip and pin and stitch my SEAMLESS GARMENT.

———

G came into the cafe with his black guitar case. I introduced him. He shook hands with many nods and smiles. He almost bowed. It made me think of a Japanese woman I once saw near the Louvre asking directions of a local. When the Parisian had finished his explanation, the woman put her hands together at the waist and bowed low in gratitude. I was as shocked as if I'd seen someone walking down the street in a suit of armour.

———

HG: 'I saw your ex last night at a party. I went up to him and we shook hands. I realised I didn't hate him as much as I thought I did.'

Ex-wife: 'Huh. You'd hate him all right if you heard what he said to me yesterday. He said he was going to destroy my life.'

———

Labor got in. Fraser wept. As if to enlighten or celebrate, the ABC ran *The Dismissal* on TV. How weird, the shadowy resemblances of actors to real people. They're a stiff-faced, stiff-necked mob, Australian politicians. Bill Hunter as Rex Connor, minister for minerals and energy—his stolid bitterness after a political life in Opposition, his grinding determination, his unpolished speech and crude social manner, his slow, sour bulk. Fraser—it's all in the way he tilts his head back and looks down his nose.

———

I watched the beginning of *La Règle du jeu* on video. It's marvellous but I've never been able to sit still long enough to get to the end. Renoir's love of people, that unfashionable thing: the sense of a rich, three-dimensional, teeming life away there beyond the flat screen and spreading out from it in all directions. A kind of fizzing and bubbling that goes on. Everyone busy living.

———

At three in the afternoon the Vietnamese schoolkids sail past my window on bicycles. 'How, how,' they cry, with their singing intonation. I can't see them but their voices float between the high houses.

———

Two wretched little urchins of eight or nine, in the doctor's rooms, one of them waiting for an X-ray. They charged in and out, communicating in grunts and foul language. A young woman came in with a tiny girl, just learning to stumble about in her nappy, knitted dress and topknot ribbon. The boys went quiet at once and approached her reverently. 'Dad-da,' she said. 'Da-da!' they repeated, beaming round at the other patients. They passed her smooth, blocky little body from one to another, tenderly helped her to walk and to get up when she fell. Everyone in the room became happy.

———

Barry Dickins made us sick with laughter remembering Lou Richards on TV. 'Some vain young footballer's up there, from Geelong probably, talking about his future, and suddenly in comes Lou Lou and whacks this great packet of bacon down on the table and yells out, "Here's some bacon for ya, compliments of Huttons—and some pantihose for the missus!"'

———

Mum had seen *Staying On* before, and was keen for me to watch it with her. Scenes of Trevor Howard and Celia Johnson sitting at a table on a terrace with their backs to mountains so wondrous… Their terrible emotional strangulation, his, in particular; she, at least, used to dance and twirl about the house, when he went out.

———

My father drove at speed along the Great Ocean Road. I hunched in the back seat, expecting to be steamrolled with horror at the sight of the burnt-out landscape, but like all such perverse hopes it was disappointed. Perhaps we were moving too fast. Perhaps I'd already seen too much of it on TV while it was actually happening, or it was too long after the event. Perhaps it had nothing to do with me and I didn't really care. The thing that did strike me was the apparent deadness of the soil itself between the black, leafless trunks. Like radioactive dust.

I spoke at the anti-nuclear rally. I hated it, felt awkward, had no idea whether the crowd could even hear me. Somewhere a jackhammer was going rat-a-tat-tat. Whenever I looked up from my notes I saw thousands and thousands of faces turned in my direction, as small as mushrooms and completely unreadable. I was boring them. My tone was pitched wrong. I became very flushed. I scrambled down off the truck. An Aboriginal bloke in dark glasses hugged me and hopped up to go next. He stuck his hands in his pockets, thrust out his chin, and became a demagogue. He laid out a series of positions and gave cues for rousing applause, which he got. I skulked away, envious but also relieved, as if let off from future duty: I'll never have to do *that* again—'climb on a wagonette to scream'.

The GP told me about a post-mortem done on some kids killed in a car smash. The pathologist had been astonished at the number of intestinal parasites they were carrying. While she was telling me this story my eye wandered to a framed photo on the wall behind her: a class of forty white-coated medical students in rows, each one holding a tiny, swaddled baby.

In *Paris Review*, an interview with James Thurber. He talked about a bulldog he once had, which used to drag rails around, six, eight, twelve feet long. He loved to get the enormous thing by the middle and try to haul it through the garden gate—'everything finely balanced, then *crash*, he'd come up against the gate posts'. This, said Thurber, was the feeling he got when reading Henry James.

The fat man in the cafe saw through the window that his Citroën was about to be booked. He sprang up, lumbered to the door, and tried to clown his way out of it. He advanced towards the parking attendant with his hands clasped behind his back and a bouncing, knee-bending gait, like a naughty child faking repentance. She looked up at him with a stony face. He dropped it and started to argue. She ignored him and kept writing. He got into the car and made as if to drive off. She tried to push the ticket through the half-open window, but he screwed it up, shoved it back at her and roared away, leaving the pink leaf fluttering on the road at her feet. 'Why should he be able to bludge in a cafe,' said F, 'while she has to work all over Easter?'

———

I feel, when I'm with him, that I'm holding myself lightly in check.

———

A wonderful night out dancing. 'As soon as they started to play,' said B, 'you knew why they existed. Every band's up there for a different reason—they were up there because they can really play guitar.' We drank whisky and champagne, and threw up on the way home. I wasn't too far gone to hold her hair.

———

Walking up Bourke Street past the Southern Cross we passed a youthful couple engaged in a fight. The bloke had his back to us but the girl was turned our way, sobbing out loud, completely without shame. Her face was distorted and tear-stained. One felt immediately on her side, that she was a good person. 'Why do you have to tell me on a fucking *street corner*,' she cried out, 'that you're—' We passed at speed. We heard a light scuffle behind us, and then a blow. We thought she'd struck him across the face, but it might have been an open hand hitting a raincoat sleeve.

———

I ripped through Katherine Mansfield's journals and letters. Flashes of rage at her for being so *cute*—the nursery tone, the sugary 'my mountains'—it turns my stomach. But it's only a protective layer over the real stuff, which is sheer muscle.

When I was not yet 'a writer' I used to write colossal, twenty-page letters to people. Now I communicate on the backs of postcards. This thought made me feel quite cheerful, as if I had imperceptibly, over years, and not by the exercise of will, rechannelled wasted energy into a more useful course—but now I mess with the taps, I keep them turned off, or let just a tiny trickle escape. I'm terribly restless and cranky, unable to be calm enough to think properly about the matter in hand, which is Philip and his daughter in the cafe.

Tiberio came into the cafe and reported that Mario in the pasta shop had just cut the top of his finger off.

Goodness I am *drunk*. Can hardly write. And while I danced I felt so *sensible*! A BOY of twenty or so and I exchanged looks as we danced beside each other. He was six foot tall with short-cropped hair and a white T-shirt. When the music was over he said to me, 'See you!' I saw Paul Madigan leaning against a speaker box at the back. I approached to shake his hand. He had not shaved.

I went to the dentist. Perhaps it was the hangover but I felt my jaw and mouth trembling with the strain of gaping. Although I didn't suffer actual pain, I felt violated, and upset.

The magazine editor damns my story with faint praise: 'Yes...I quite liked it actually...the dialogue works...in parts...' I hung up the phone in embarrassment and confusion. And then I wrote him a letter that was like a hard kick in the arse.

I hereby resolve to refuse all social engagements on weekdays (before evening) from now on. I am completely out of synch and it'll take me weeks to get back in.

People sometimes talk about their boredom and I don't know what they mean. But this afternoon I had a nap, longer than necessary, and woke to find it was raining and no one had brought the clothes in off the line. I went downstairs and began to do the ironing. On the radio was some oboe music, full of formal resignation, and I started to feel those old waves of sadness, as if outside the house were nothing but grey wet fields and other buildings made of grey wet stone and people in clumsy, ugly clothes and strange hats.

In the car on the way to the restaurant last night with the visiting American lefties, I heard myself talking smoothly, putting on an effortless, tailored, hard-nosed little performance for their benefit. Disgusted, I fell silent. At the table I mentioned the name of Italo Calvino. Everyone looked at me blankly. I sat there full of anxiety. I'm finished as a writer, irredeemably bourgeois, my concerns so small (waiters in a cafe, a girl kneeling on a bed singing 'Lush Life'). All I've got are those ten pages in my room. This morning I got to my office and took it into my head to make a plan. What a sudden revolution then occurred! I rushed out and bought some system cards, wrote a character's name on each one, and pinned them up in a horizontal row. I thought very hard, pacing up and down and dashing off notes and reassuring statements, for an hour. Then, just as suddenly, the rush faltered and was over. I locked the door and went to see *Sophie's Choice*. Too pretty. Two prams exquisitely arranged by the railway tracks. And don't people vomit when they've taken cyanide?

'I have spent an hour cooking this meal. I would like you to eat it with a less foul-tempered look on your face.'

———

I saw Princess Diana go past in a Rolls-Royce. Such a *pretty* girl.

———

I hadn't seen the former actor for a couple of years. In the cafe he told me he was in love. 'Because I'm a fairly gentle sort of bloke—because I've been thoroughly trained by feminists—well, I've got this power to really *blow people away*.' He smiled, breathing out audibly through his nose. 'What do we all look like?' he went on luxuriously. He glanced down at my sober, dull clothes. 'You—you could be a school teacher. *I*—'

'You look like what you are,' said another man at the table. 'A fucking arts bureaucrat from Sydney.'

———

The impervious self-confidence of the upper-middle-class educated young Frenchman. That smooth, slightly bilious skin, the narrow, pretty mouth, the small chin, the bony nose, the large intelligent eyes. He talks and talks, completely unaware that his concern at having reached the age of twenty-five is of no interest to anyone.

———

The bitter, sadistic-looking waiter in Notturno approached me today and said, 'I think I wrote something beautiful. Will you pass judgment on it for me?' He had recorded it on cassette, and gave it to me to take away. It consists largely of philosophical dissertations of a nebulous kind. The effect of his badly recorded voice is distressing, almost moving, because the pauses and silences are so eloquent.

———

In a caravan park on the western outskirts of Sydney some people noticed a dazed-looking man standing by his caravan in blood-soaked clothes. They called the police. He has been charged with the murder of a man found clubbed to death with a hammer—and with frightful attacks on three young teachers, women, who worked at a school for retarded children and were asleep in their quarters. He broke in, forced one of the women to tie up the other two, and made them torture each other, then hacked two of them to death. The third one survived to tell the tale. On TV, very sober, quiet shots of what looked like a small country town: a road leading to a building with a faded green corrugated-iron roof.

———

I can't write any more. I'm clumsy. Outside my window a fine rain is falling, perfectly vertical.

———

An article about different translations of Baudelaire's poem *La Cloche fêlée*. I read the poem out loud to myself and got one of those shocks that only poetry can deliver: a violent shiver, a rush of tears. I took off my hat to Richard Howard who, in his urge to render the last three lines, shows the poet in himself with a string of verbs: 'the gasping of a wounded soldier left/ beside a lake of blood, who, pinned beneath/ a pile of dead men, struggles, stares and dies.' But of course the original is somewhere else, that last line so strange and horrible: '*Et qui meurt, sans bouger, dans d'immenses efforts.*'

———

The biographer came over. We talked about writing. She said she'd started reading *The White Hotel* but when she got to a description of an old woman in a ditch having a bayonet shoved up her cunt, she closed the book. 'These days,' she said, 'it's considered a mark of moral superiority to contemplate the most horrible things. *I* think it's a sickness, the mark of an inadequate intellect. That's why I'm *sick* of Tolstoy, and think he's inferior to Henry James—because he won't admit the possibility of freedom.' He won't? I had nothing to say about this. I realise that I accept blindly what I read.

Three young men, whose catamaran was wrecked on the North Queensland coast, struggled for three days through mangroves so thick that it took them two hours to go two hundred yards.
Woman interviewer: 'But you had no water.'

Man: 'We licked dew off leaves.'

Interviewer: 'How did you have the energy to keep going, with no food?'

Man: (*with a small snuffle of laughter*) 'Aw, I dunno. Hope…I s'pose…'

After dinner the power went off and the house was dark. We sat quietly by the fire talking about syntax and whether it was snobbery and a misuse of power to criticise the mangling of it. She opined that Murray Bail did not put that split infinitive in the first line of *Homesickness* on purpose. He didn't even know, she said.

'*Tsk*. Why are you crying?'

'In Blanche d'Alpuget's book someone is crying and a kid asks why. The mother says, "Because there is bitterness in life." That's why I'm crying.'

'*Pfff*. That's just literature. I'm cold.'

'You're saying cold things. That's why you're cold.'

'I'm cold because I'm thinking.'

'Can't you think and feel at the same time?'

'No.'

G talks about telling his daughter he's leaving. 'I'm grief-laden,' he says. 'I walk round laden with grief.' He's standing very straight, with his back against the street window of Notturno, like a man facing a firing squad.

Within two minutes I was sobbing and F was out of the room. I wanted to punch my hand through the window, smash up the house, I wanted to hurt myself, I couldn't feel it enough, I was looking for pain. I bashed the wall with my fists. He heard my racket and came back, put his arms around me stiffly, made me get into bed and tucked me in, kissed my cheek and left quietly like a mother hoping a sick kid is about to drop off to sleep and give her some peace. He had put the doona on sideways. My feet were sticking out. When the door closed I had to get out of bed, snivelling, and turn the whole thing around.

———

I have decided to smarten up my appearance. I bought some pretty earrings, and I now have two dresses. With woollen tights and my ankle boots from Paris I feel a killer of style.

———

'What's the matter?' Nothing major, but I don't like being reminded of the fact that I don't look happy.

———

I wonder if I could write a play. I can *imagine* a play. It will be about different points of view of exactly the same event. She comes in and they're at the kitchen table drinking. 'Do you want a sherry?' 'Yes.' 'There isn't any left.' 'Well why the fuck did you ask me then?' There would be different starting points, e.g. the boot-throwing scene.

———

Mount Buffalo. Folds and folds of 'armèd hills', blue after blue, and a cold wind rushing up from a deep gorge as it got dark—a roaring which might have been air in leaves or else a white, thin, steep torrent that I thought I saw half a mile below. A lyrebird strolled past me on its large feet, among the granite boulders. I shuffled, to alert it, but it glanced up casually and kept walking.

I tried to buy a coat. The only one I liked was Italian, marked down from $999 to $333. But it did not fit me. I bought a slip, a pair of black tights, a ream of A4, some carbon paper, and two pencil sharpeners.

My old teacher invited me to lunch at University House. He is tiny, plumpish, pink and grey, silver-haired, with soft, unwhiskered skin on his cheeks, as if he never needs to shave. He is a keen talker, a skilled and funny storyteller, a gossip, I suppose—not exactly malicious, but hard: 'They were tough with him and he went to water. I rang him up. I said, "What do you want done?" He said, "No, nothing. It's all right." He was going to get back in their good books by showing them he was a good boy.' Ouch. 'She must have known when she married him that she was condemning herself to the six kids, the whole family thing.'

The famously gloomy Stalinist had cut his hair very very short and 'started a new relationship'. He looked almost cheerful.

'What's your book about, Hels?'

'Oh…love, pain…'

'Interview *me*.'

'Everything you know about pain, my dear, you have already told me.'

'I've learnt something else.'

'What?'

'I've learnt that some things are beyond words.'

'Didn't you always know that?'

'No. I thought everything could be intellectualised.'

'Well, that's an advance, isn't it?'

'Except that it can make a pessimist even more pessimistic.'

'But if all that was standing between you and sheer pessimism was a false belief, isn't it better to—'

He laughed and turned away. 'Yeah, yeah, course, it's better.'

I made a plan: in the mornings I'll try to write my book, and in the afternoons I'll work on the translations of the Malraux programs for SBS. I started this morning at 8 am. I loved it in my room, quiet all around, barely even properly light. I rewrote Vicki and Elizabeth, the very beginning of the book. I worry that I ought to pour out a whole draft and then go back and rewrite. What I do is write a page, then fix it up straight away and go back to the beginning to see if everything fits. So my progress is slow. But the work is solid. After lunch I sat at my desk with the big dictionaries, the mild afternoon sun on my back through the window, and wrestled away. Writing in the morning is battling through jungle. Translating in the arvo is riding along a flat country road on a bicycle.

These mornings we see the most dazzling sunrises: the five cypress trees I can see from my bedroom window point like a raised hand in front of a broad band of clear sky with dove-grey cloud, pink-tinged, above it. Birds sing loudly. I don't know where they are.

Every day when I sit down at the desk I wonder if there will come a certain moment when, with a pop, each character will attain physical reality in my imagination, quite separate from its worldly model.

We used to be friends but now I'm afraid of him. The photo on the back of his new book shows him black-faced, black-browed, his shirtsleeves rolled up to show strangler's arms, all muscly and hairy.

How am I going to survive this? I have a lemming-like urge to dash off the cliff now, instead of waiting till he leaves. It's like the urge to punch walls: 'Look how you hurt me. I am acting out a little play of pain.'

———

I like making cosmic observations, e.g. the power enjoyed by those who ride in the back seats of cars.

———

The only way I can keep a rhythm going is to keep off booze, go to bed early, and not drink too much coffee. 8.30–12.30 work on novel in office. 2.00–4.00 translate at home. 7.30–10.00 read Vogel Award manuscripts at home. Most of them are unbelievably terrible. One was like a black hole in space: all my energy was sucked into it, it drained and sucked and gave back no spark. It scared me.

———

I went to a union meeting. God, it was boring, stacked with old dead-heads obsessed with procedure. A man I used to teach with in the seventies shyly expressed to me his disappointment: he had expected the meeting to be 'about literature'.

———

O was down from Sydney. We went for a long walk in the cemetery. I asked him about a woman we knew at university. He told me that she had jumped off a building. He said she had remade herself, after a terrible car crash in which she had sustained brain damage, but it wasn't good enough for her and it wasn't going to get any better. So she jumped. We agreed that this was consistent with her whole life and personality: reckless courage.

———

G wrote to me, speaking of heroin, coke, a 'suicide' attempt by his girlfriend. She scratched her wrists with a pin, 'then asked me to hit her up with heroin. I did, then had some myself.' Disgusting confidences. Nothing he can do will surprise me, but I thought she was tougher, clever, going somewhere.

———

'I met a man,' said U, 'and we talked about you. He said that he found you a very interesting person; that he thought you were shy; and that you were not going to let people waste your time.' I wondered what she had said in reply, but did not ask.

———

'When you say you cough blood, what do you mean exactly? Is it just a pinkish tinge, or—you don't mean actual gouts, do you?'
    'Yeah, gouts,' said G. 'Black. Especially in the morning.'

———

We fought about housework. I saw red and smashed a plate and a bowl.
    'There are more plates here. Why don't you break them as well?'
    'Shut your face.'
    He went upstairs and turned the TV on full blast. I swept up the mess. I bawled a lot as I swept, and then as I washed my plain, spotty, forty-year-old face and looked at it in the mirror and thought that I couldn't bear having to go through another bout of this BATTLING. I also thought, I am about to get my period. It absolutely *shits* me that this should explain anything. I objectively do most of the housework and it's NOT FAIR. After I'd washed my face I took off my pants and they were stained black with blood.

———

This flaming book is jammed again. I feel my ignorance and fear like a vast black hole.

———

Heading for Griffith University in the Kombi. At nightfall I walked down the main street of Gundagai eating hot chips out of newspaper. The lumpy little hill straight ahead of me was dead black, its silhouette fringed with the odd gum. The fading light behind it, airy, mauve and pure, seemed to be projected upwards towards two horizontal streaks of grey cloud. In my motel room the double bed sank in the middle before I even got into it. A deep sleep. Dreams of Paris: climbing flights of stairs. I peeped out at dawn and saw darkness, and thick frost on the Kombi's windscreen. How comforting it is to write in this notebook, in an awful room so far from home. I write, and become lord of all I survey.

She kissed me goodbye. Her firm cool cheek: still a child's slight plumpness. Poppy's will be like that, to Elizabeth. I thought a lot on the Hume highway about how to make Elizabeth an unlikeable character but still interesting.

Woman in the hippie gift shop. About fifty, blonde, a weather-beaten, upper-class face with piercing blue eyes. 'I'm asexual,' she announced. 'I've been wanting to talk to someone about this. I don't have a relationship with a man, and I *love* my life.'

ABC radio is a wonderful institution for travellers and other solitary people: those soothing talk programs full of information about echidnas. Apparently the echidna, the hedgehog and the porcupine each evolved quite separately.

In the restaurant it was 'go to the counter and get it yourself'. I was out of place, the only solitary among the families and the groups of young people hardly out of childhood, smoking desperately between mouthfuls. Perched on bar stools four women in their late twenties were sipping wine and smiling, smiling, smiling at each other as their conversation went. I wondered whether my loneliness made me want to take notes, or vice versa: how is a writer made?

R says that in reading she is always looking for the moral voice of the writer. She says she never feels better after having committed violence—not even after smashing a plate.

'I do,' I said defiantly.

'I don't,' she repeated. A pause.

'I'm not sure if I do or not,' I said. 'I feel humiliated when I have to sweep up the pieces.'

The seven-year-old is a jolly, endearing boy. He described someone as 'greedy and boastful'. I said, 'Is it boastful to tell about one's successes? I remember you boasting once that you were the second-best runner in your school.'

'Second-best *long distance* runner! And that wasn't boasting! That was a *success*!'

I dreamt that my publisher told me my novel was bad. 'Bad? Why?' 'Oh yes. It's terrible.' Through my waking mind ran escape clauses: I'll do short stories instead; she mustn't have liked the trimmed-back style; I'll take out the old man's hairy hands. I was panicking, but deep down I was not surprised.

D, who I'm billeted with, seems to believe, as do many people who are fully-fledged examples of their type, that she is 'not like' the others: 'I can't stand academics,' she says. 'I was born not standing academics.' And yet she has their brittle manner, their tendency to monologue, their habit of irony, of picking up words in tweezers. I'd better look out. No one's safe, once they've been inside a university.

Awfully homesick. I walked for miles along a beach. On my way back I saw a foreign man who had found an orange fish floundering in the shallows, and was trying to flip it into deeper water with his thong. I ran forward and picked it up by the tail, but it flipped strongly—I'd never picked up a live fish before and was astonished by its muscle—I had to seize it in two hands and fling it out to sea. 'Sank you, sank you,' cried the man and his two female companions.

I went to a lecture on realism. A lot of detached, ironic descriptions were offered, in a tone that seemed to assume that realism is historically discredited now and rather dull. I don't know if I'm a realist or not. I don't think it's a good idea to sit around in a university trying to categorise myself. The lecturer said twice that words signify reality but don't represent it. I'd quite like to find out what this means, but I'm not breaking my neck.

I worked all morning, slipping myself slowly back into the world of the book. I love Athena. She is rather stern. I'm dying to make her meet Philip. They will have dry kisses that lead nowhere.

In the campus bookshop I accidentally stole something. The woman at the register was cold and rude to me, quite unnecessarily, and I left the shop in irritable confusion. Halfway back to the Humanities building I realised I was still carrying Elizabeth Bowen's *The Last September*. Fuck you, I thought, and kept walking.

In this town the rubbish man comes right into the backyard, finds your bin wherever it may stand, and heaves its contents into another bin that he carries on his shoulders.

An Englishman invited me to a class about technique. 'You're a writer. You might be interested.' He gave me the course outline and said to come at four. I read it and was alarmed to see that it had nothing whatsoever to do with any sense of the word *technique* that I'd ever heard of. I had no idea what he was getting at. I went, miserably, to his class. He talked for an hour and I still had very little clue. It all seemed so cloudy, so full of terms I did not know. My spirits sank and sank. Later I tried to explain my response to two academics I met at dinner. They were amused and encouraging. I said, 'I feel inadequate, and as though I'm under attack.' 'You probably are,' said the man. 'Not in a personal way, but your assumptions are being challenged.' I suppose it's good for me, but I still don't see any link between the lecturer's 'technique' and what I do in my notebook.

———

Another Englishman (the place is swarming with them) lent me some Roland Barthes: 'to show you he's weally about w'iting'. I read a little piece called *La Lumière du Sud-Ouest*. It was beautiful. Hills '*toutes proches et violettes*'.

———

The Italian academic said she hated this town and had not gone to any other places in Australia, although she's been here nearly four years.

    HG: (*shocked*) 'But why?'

    Woman: (*with an eloquent grimace and a sideways flicking gesture*) 'Every time I had holidays I just couldn't *stand* it here, so I'd go back to Rome.'

    I found this so mortifying I almost burst into tears. I was the only Australian at the table and I was terribly offended.

———

On many mornings in this house a radio alarm clicks on in the kitchen at 6.30. No one ever gets up in response to it. I feel guilty, as if I had set it myself. I get up and stand on the cold floor, unable to decide whether I should switch it off or not.

———

F calls me from his parents' house, where he's taken M on a visit. 'I suddenly understand,' he says, 'why I get so mad with you when you're bossy. It's *very* bossy here.'

A long interview-documentary with Billy Wilder, a charming and likeable old rogue who, in the final ten minutes, turned on the interviewer, a humourless French film buff with the appropriate name of Michel Ciment, and made gentle mockery of him: 'The only thing worse than not being taken seriously, Michel, is being taken too seriously. As long as I can make movies, I don't give a shit.'

My sister told me that a young man had come off his motorbike last night outside her holiday apartment at Surfers. In the paper this morning his death was reported. 'I heard the crash,' she said, 'and I ran out to see if it was the girls. He was lying with his helmet near him, it had flown off, and his head was right up against the gutter. There was quite a bit of blood. As soon as I saw it wasn't the girls I thought, There's plenty of people looking after him, and I went inside and got back into bed.'

Up here I'm little more than a machine that records horrors and small dismays.

'The best thing you can do as a Creative Writing teacher,' said a man who had been one for four years, 'is to put tight fences around them. I used to tell them I was absolutely not interested in their outpourings. It's worth it. At the end you say, Well, X came in here a verbal cripple, and he's walking out the door without crutches.'

'I love you,' said G on the phone, vaguely, as if wanting to register a small fact while the occasion presented itself. I knew that already.

It's part of what I know about the world, but it's never steady, it flickers and disappears, and I would only feel this as painful if I'd been steering myself by its unreliable light. This metaphor will stand, if I don't try to develop it any further.

———

The Vogel judging in Sydney was pure pleasure. We were put in an office high above bits of harbour, with windows that didn't open. It seemed that I hadn't laughed out loud in the company of others since I left Melbourne. (Frank Moorhouse: 'Beware of committees that laugh too much.')

———

In the pub, as the priest waited for me to finish with the public phone, he took a few steps back into the lounge where a jukebox was playing some loud rocking thing. He turned his back to me, unaware that I was watching him through the glass door, and took three big steps in time to the music, swinging out his arms in a large, free gesture, embracing the world. I like men. I just *like* them. (But not Norman Mailer.)

———

If I lived in Sydney perhaps these people, and the women they know, would be my friends. Perhaps this is just a provincial fantasy. Perhaps their lives are as closed as mine sometimes seems to be, in Melbourne.

———

I wiped myself and saw blood. Days early. Cynicism says: a disease. Romance says: weeping.

———

I wondered, seeing the state G was in, whether I did agree after all with his remark about the attractiveness of other people's unhappiness. I wanted to sweep out his head with a straw broom, wash out his mouth with soap, put him across my knee and spank him with a rolled-up newspaper, and then fuck him silly, just to cheer him up. Instead we walked along a path in a park, looked at the Opera House gleaming in the sunshine, and felt extremely patriotic.

———

Frank O'Hara is a ratbag, so likeable, and what a voice. 'Love's life-giving vulgarity,' he says in his ridiculous Manifesto.

———

A house! The sun comes in/ Through small surprising windows./ The occupants left for the coast/ early this morning in an old car./ 'Sleep in our bed,' they said,/ and I will: I've made it up already/ with thin blankets out of a cupboard./ I've turned back the top corner/ And placed the pillow;/ But that's for later. Now/ I cut my fingernails to the quick/ And sit down at the piano, giddy,/ The child all secret left alone/ With bare board and kitchen jars,/ Doors that don't lock, And ragged bleached towels/ Which have drunk water off those/ Travelling bodies that I love.

It took me an hour and a half to write that. The whole time I was reworking it I was thinking I should be doing something else. I'll never be a poet! But it's more fun than prose, that's for sure.

———

Opposite the bedroom window stands a church. The morning light brightens its sandstone steeple. Pigeons swagger along its edges.

———

'Want to come with us to see *Flashdance?*'
 'Love to! Only one problem—if it's tomorrow I might be going to the Opera House to see *The Cherry Orchard.*'
 'It's fabulous! You'll cry! No, you won't *cry*...'
 'Yes I will. You should've seen me at *Three Sisters.*'

———

'I saw she had been writing you a postcard,' wrote B, 'and I was full of jealousy. I thought, Well, if everyone else is going to write to her,

I'm not. These feelings must be hounded out and whipped like a thieving servant boy.'

———

The young girl's confident vocabulary: 'If you look at her hands fleetingly you don't even notice; but if you examine them properly…'

———

Been drinking again. But all I had was three margaritas and one very watered-down scotch. So I am all right.

———

Missed the plane. Do not care. Walk with slow steps in my pink high-heeled sandals. The muzak in the airport sounds as if it's being boiled, or percolated. One is not sure what tune it is, though it causes a familiar feeling.

———

A student brought me a poem she had written. She asked me to correct her punctuation. The first line: 'A, TV reporter came up to him.'

———

One of the Englishmen grumbles fiercely to me at lunch about the 'theory' people in the department. He's furious because they make their students read theory of literary criticism without reading the novels first. 'I was interested when they said they were going to teach *Lady Chatterley's Lover* and the trial. I thought, They'll have to read the novel. But they didn't. They studied the transcript of the trial.' I'm listening, agog, but just as what he's shouting becomes really interesting, he breaks off mid-sentence. 'Why did you stop talking?' 'I've got high blood pressure.' 'What? Don't be silly.' 'No, it's true. And there are better things to get worked up about.'

———

While the GP was writing out my prescription, she was breast-feeding her baby.

We lay on the couches in his living room, gossiping about musicians.

'She's got no studio manners,' said G.

'What's that mean?'

'Okay. We're in this very small room. She's holding a guitar, I'm not. I'm in there trying to tell her how to do it. The guitar is connected. The slightest flutter she makes on the strings makes a tremendous noise. I say, "How about trying it like this?" She goes chucka-chucka-chucka—gets it wrong—and in her frustration she *whacks* the strings, really hard. The noise it makes is like being punched in the head! I nearly have to cover my ears! It *hurts*! And she does this ten, fifteen times!'

The evening comes down. A postcard I'd left on the bed in the morning was bent in a curve. Crickets make their soothing, reliable rhythm. A visible mistiness fills the valley. The house is like a ship: riding high in damp air.

On TV, riot police in Santiago, Chile charge a peaceful sit-in against the military regime: they savagely attack students with their nightsticks. A witness says, 'They fell to the ground, blood gushed from their heads, the man was screaming in agony, his head was dented like a ping pong ball.' People all over the city toot their car horns in protest, and people inside their houses, when night falls, begin to beat spoons against saucepans. The whole city is in uproar.

I'm worried about art, what it's for, whether what I do is any use to anyone, whether I've been kidding myself all these years that I'm any good at it, that I've got anything at all to offer the human race, whether I should just chuck it in and look for a job.

I was astonished at the violence of the short story. The control the writer thinks he has of it is the control that a furiously angry driver has of a car, a person who ought to be kept from the wheel until he recovers his temper: the narrative voice makes grinding changes, throws itself into sickening halts and turns. The last few sentences are a head hitting the windscreen.

———

When the Englishman washes the dishes he splashes water all down his front in great slops that soak his shirt and trousers. He is perfectly oblivious, for he is singing to me, in a sweet and cultivated light tenor, a song to illustrate why he loves Berlioz. We show each other photos of our children, whom we painfully miss. 'She looks wise,' he says, looking at M, and she does: thin arms folded over the sinewy torso, the straight line of the mouth, the eyes with their reserved, humorous expression.

———

The student and I sat together at the kitchen table, sewing. She was taking in a pair of trousers; I was mending the sleeve of a dress.

'This is nice, isn't it,' I said. 'Reminds me of that scene in *Gone With the Wind* where the women sit sewing while the men are out getting into trouble.'

'And,' she said, 'one of them is reading out loud from *David Copperfield*. "Chaptah One. Ah am bawn."'

———

At the hippies' house for dinner, I find in my slice of quiche two foreign items: a dead match and a pubic hair. I hide them under a lettuce leaf and we go on talking.

———

At the prize-giving I stretch out my legs and rest my feet on a kind of wooden pew. A journalist from Sydney called K introduces himself, sits on my feet and tells me several gaudy tales of his emotional life:

various insane behaviours. I feel like taking the cheeky-faced fellow by the hand, leading him into a dark hallway, and saying, 'Let's kiss.' I discipline myself by planning a Schnitzler-style short story about the waxing and waning of a flirtation. By the time I get home I have forgotten it.

———

A Christian student came to see me and talked at length about her decision to leave university. 'I'd been praying about it for a long time. In church last Sunday I got an answer. I knew that I had to leave. The Lord spoke to me. He said, "Well, are you going to serve me, or aren't you?"' I was interested in what she said. I did not think it was silly. I imagine that if one became a Christian one could not do otherwise than to proselytise. Anything else would be inconsistent.

———

My predecessor in the department talked to me in confidence about D. He has known her for many years. Everything he said confirmed my own doubts and suspicions. Still, I feel an allegiance to her which makes this disloyal scribbling seem treacherous—a cold, slightly sickened sensation of curiosity which, when I pick up the pen and the diary, presents itself almost as a duty: isn't this what writers *do*? Can a writer be a loyal friend? To be a loyal friend I'd have to mark off a distinct line past which I decline to make mental notes, to probe or observe.

———

The dog in the house over the back has been circling it for an hour or so, barking to be let in. I can feel my shoulders going rigid. I wish I could make a tremendous *noise*. If I had a gun I'd fire it into the air until they came out and shut him up.

———

Before dinner, three little boys of charm and vigour clumsily handed round plates of biscuits and pâté. Their father winced and flinched at their awkwardness. He made them go to their room. Twenty minutes later the middle one came out in tears. He stood on the lounge-room carpet in his cotton shortie pyjamas and absolutely howled. 'What's the matter?' said his mother. 'Dad won't let me out!' he bawled, fat tears bouncing off his cheeks. 'Oh, let him out,' she said to her husband. 'He's *so* sociable.'

———

Two men listen to Strauss's *Four Last Songs*.

'I hate sleep,' said one. 'Sleep is death.'

'That,' said the other, 'has something to do with why your marriage broke up.'

———

My clever student has the 500-watt blue eyes, black-lashed and set ever so slightly too close together, that cause the person on whom they rest to feel a significance he almost certainly does not intend.

———

I've started a story called 'Postcards from Surfers'. If I can maintain the tone, and keep it all small and bare, it will be good. I know I'll never write anything that could be called 'great'. I suppose for that you have to have a big idea. All my ideas are small and the best I can do is cobble them together.

———

My sister told me that being with our parents made her cry. When she woke in the morning after their visit her eyes were so puffy that she looked 'like a cane toad'.

———

The board member astonished me by her vehemence against the funding of poets. She went right overboard, deckchairs and all, laughing as she spoke. She said she rarely read poetry and that most poets were full of shit, posturing and squabbling among themselves. I thought of R, the only poet I know, quietly and patiently spinning away in secret, and wondered if the board member had any idea (or if I did myself) of the length of that process, compared with the job of prose. She seemed to think that poetry could be dashed off in the gaps between real activities. Well, perhaps it can, but what about the long, slow formation of something big, or pure?

―――

G asked me to visit him at the studio. He kept me waiting for half an hour, then told me a tale of how he'd behaved on Saturday night: 'I made a real animal of myself.' I listened, with the weary, unjudging curiosity his stories provoke in me. He had locked himself in a bedroom at a party with the wife of his friend; not only was his official girlfriend also at the party, the one he'd left his wife for, but some other 'new girlfriend' with whom, unbeknownst to the official one, he had just spent the afternoon. Having related this to me, he went to a different part of the building and didn't come back. I finished reading the paper, listened to a small orchestra in the next studio, and left without saying goodbye.

―――

I'm scared to go to my office in case I can't make things up.

―――

I wrote two or three sentences about Vicki waking up. Vicki is the only character who is almost completely invented. I love to let her float around in my mind, bumping up against things that are in there: views, articles of furniture.

―――

I would like to make Elizabeth *hard*. She is already but I have this sneaking romantic duty to show a soft side to her—as if she is 'really' just as 'vulnerable' as anyone else, only hides it better. A scene where she will shock Athena with her bitterness and pessimism.

―――

Dreamt that G betrayed me. He robbed me of my bag, and blatantly admitted it. I woke from this dream knowing, before I even opened my eyes, what it meant: that I felt *I* was betraying and robbing *him*, by writing a character that's based on him. But I can't stop now.

———

'Your school shoes are disgusting. Why don't you clean them?'
 'It's fashionable to have dirty shoes.'

———

F buys a house, a tiny dump, all crooked but nice. He is going to live in it by himself. He has doubts. 'What will I do after work?'
 Me: (*briskly*) 'You'll drive home to your place, have a sleep and a wash, then you'll ring us and say, "Can I come over?" and I'll say, "Do you want to come for tea?"'

———

I loved the scene in Syberberg's film of *Parsifal* where Klingsor summons Kundry from sleep and urges her to try to seduce Parsifal. He asks her what she wants and she cries out, 'Sleep! Everlasting sleep!' Each time one of these bloody men revives her or drags her out, she opens her eyes in a kind of horror, like a failed suicide who comes back to consciousness, looks around and says, 'Oh *no*—I'm *still alive*.'

———

I don't enjoy the way the therapist fixes me with her unblinking gaze. She seems to want to urge me to undertake a search and reconstruction of myself such as the one she herself is attempting. When I think of her ugly clothes and the quite stunning, almost deathly ugliness of the inside of her house I shiver. She is trying to get me to face the most difficult area in myself. I don't have the courage to do it. Not now, anyway. Thinking about it is like contemplating a mountain range in winter.

———

I do feel sad though at the way the sun passes unobstructed through his empty room.

On the tram home M and I examined together the intro to a book of Scarlatti sonatas. It quoted a sentence in archaic language. I began to read it out loud (not very). 'Helen!' she said, twisting her shoulders. '*Shhhh!*' I felt, as always when she is embarrassed by my public demeanour, stabbed to the heart. I turned my face away and sat very still. 'What's the matter?' 'I hate it when you tell me to shut up. It makes me feel awful.' 'I didn't tell you to shut up!' In the house later each of us went about her business, but I noticed that when our paths crossed she smiled at me, instead of walking around in a dream as she normally does these days. When she left for her friend's place she kissed me goodbye. And last night at dinner, she actually *sat on my knee* and leaned against me for at least *ten minutes*.

A woman on the Lygon Street tram was afraid that her four- or five-year-old son would fall out through the open side of the middle section. She gripped his wrist.

'But I want to walk around.'

'No, Sam, you can't. It's dangerous.'

He bursts into a roar: 'But I *want* to!'

'You *can't*, Sam. It's *dangerous*.'

'Please let me go! Oh, please! Let me go! Let me out! *Please!*'

'No! Look! If you fell out there you'd be under those wheels and you'd be dead! *Dead!*'

'No I wouldn't! Please let me go, please, please!'

'No! I don't trust you, Sam. I don't trust you not to do something silly!'

'I won't do something silly!'

'You've been silly all morning!'

'No I haven't! I haven't been silly!'

'I don't trust you, Sam! I *don't trust* you!'

It was a neurotic drama conducted at top volume, utterly without abashment of any kind.

I was alone in the house late on a summer evening, playing the piano with all the windows open. Somebody knocked at the front door. I was seized by fear. But when I looked out the window I saw the bearded Greek. We sat at the table and drank some wine. He read me his new poems. I liked best some short ones about a Gertrude Street cafe he worked in: 'A woman crosses the road and becomes a waitress.' As he read, I watched a small moon, in a dark blue sky 'seeded with stars', sail with surprising rapidity across the uncovered window behind him.

I flipped through *The Horse's Mouth* and found a message to me: 'What I say to an artist is—WHEN YOU CAN'T PAINT, PAINT. But something else.'

I think about my characters, and their world is real to me.

I lay around all evening in my cotton nightie and watched TV by myself. The dog dreamed in her beanbag. Every now and then I got off the sofa and sprayed myself with Yardley's Lily of the Valley.

Now G tells me he's left his girlfriend and fallen in love with a woman who's 'a cross between Marilyn Monroe and…'

'Are you in the shit?'

He nods.

'What happened?'

'It's like having lived with the moon for four years, and the sun comes out.'

1984

We talked about A. S. Byatt's novel *The Virgin in the Garden*. B said she hadn't liked or been convinced by the sex between the older sister and the plump curate. 'I've never felt anything like that,' she said rather testily. I was astonished to hear this: it was the first time I'd ever read an account of those profound wanderings of the imagination that have occurred in me while I was fucking—as if my own body, blood vessels, my inner hollowness were a whole country in which I slowly and dreamily travelled—along rivers, in endless gardens—like a stage set or a mighty reddish-lit cavern.

I have drunk three glasses of chablis and feel tiddly. But I am not drunk. I know this from the fact that I have just sewn on the Singer two calico cushion covers. And they fit.

'He's mixed up with a twenty-five-year-old,' says U miserably. 'She has a Playboy body and eyes that are blue. But without depth.'

He snored, so I crept out and slept on the hard fold-out couch, wrapped in a cotton blanket. I dreamed I was in a Dickens novel, that I was happy and that I laughed and laughed. Another character 'tortured water' in his experiments. I wore a pretty muslin dress and I was in love with someone, a funny and clever man who was also kind. When I woke up my eyes were puffy and my nose was blocked, as if I had been crying for a long time.

———

The gum-tree boughs are so flexible, they toss like heads of hair.

———

Sunbaking with my sister in her garden. 'Look out, Helen, there's a very bad worm just near your foot.'

———

At the Greek restaurant our table was in a kind of annexe with a canvas roof stretched over it, filled with small flourishing trees, which dropped little mauve flowers on to our dinner. I went looking for the toilet. The upper floor was like a cheap hotel in Teheran or Cairo: an air of something sinister having just happened; rooms emptied very recently of personal belongings but still holding their former occupants' presence, like an agitating gas.

———

I'm often surprised to find, when I reread an article for which I have been criticised as harsh or unsympathetic, that my tone in the piece is quite courteous and benevolent. Even mild.

———

I thought that I ought to do more planning for this book—never leave my office without having made solid notes for the next day's work. Today I did plan, and now I feel curious as to what will surface when I sit down tomorrow and follow my own orders: 'Philip, Poppy and Elizabeth go to dinner at the Foxes' in Bunker Street'. Philip will have a very small butterfly tattoo. I want him to talk about watching a science program on TV: 'that acidy little zing'. Dexter won't know what he means by 'acidy'. I also have *major* decisions to make about *who* Athena is going to *get off with*. I can't believe she'll have enough money to go to Europe.

On the other hand, who does? Mustn't let this realism business get on top of me.

When we got to the biographer's house she spoke with exaggerated care. The grinding deliberateness of her manner was really just her ordinary tone intensified a great deal. The penny didn't drop for a while that she was profoundly drunk and trying to pretend she wasn't. To kick things along I talked about the Florence Nightingale biography I've been reading. She asked whether Nightingale remained a virgin all her life. 'I think so,' I said. 'She seems to have decided against anything other than work. Oh—she did receive several good offers of marriage—' At this she burst out laughing and turned her head away. '*Good* offers of marriage?' she repeated, with the grating bitterness she always shows whenever marriage is mentioned favourably. She went very slowly upstairs and returned a long time later with some poems, which she read to us. She said no one would publish them. If I'd been frank I'd have said, 'You're not a poet. Your poems are really prose. They're plodding, and lecturing. You haven't got a poet's imagination.' People can't *say* that kind of thing, I think.

Today I worked in a trance for nearly four hours. I did the dinner scene at the Foxes' place. I even got to the very end, when Poppy says on the way home, 'Athena's perfect, isn't she.' Dexter sings his hymn, is crossed by Vicki, falls off his chair and breaks it. They drink a whole bottle of gin. Athena and Philip notice each other. I cobbled together that scene out of elements so disparate that only a compulsive note-taker like me could have had the raw material at her disposal. Whacko! I could have gone on all day but didn't want to push my luck.

From reading Doris Lessing I saw how I might one day *dare* to exaggerate the surreal aspects, e.g. the Paradise Bar…but I let myself be distracted and did not go to my office.

———

My friend goes into her fourteen-year-old daughter's bedroom in the morning and finds her sitting up in bed with a boy, a girl in the other bed, all three of them naked and chattering away, the daughter with love bites all over her neck. 'What's going on here?' The answer to this was not reported to me.

———

I am learning not to round a scene off. I like to leave the reader with one leg hanging over the edge—like E. M. Forster: 'but her voice floated out to swell the night's uneasiness.' I am trimming so close to the bone that a reader will require either good will or sensitive nerves. Naturally I would prefer the latter.

———

At a table near me sat three or four couples in their early thirties, bogging into their lunch—the men in shorts and T-shirts, the women with neat haircuts and modest clothes. There appeared in the cafe doorway two teenaged girls, one tiny and slim, the other plumper, taller, blonder, wearing on top of her head a flamboyantly tied pink bow. One of the men spotted the bow-girl. He gaped, caught the eye of another man at his table and gave a high-pitched, exaggerated laugh, dropping his face towards his plate. His companions, both women and men, looked up and followed suit. Their mockery was so loud, so rude, so uncalled-for, that I felt a burst of furious anger. I sat there staring at them with hatred. I thought I should have walked over to the first man who had laughed and said, 'What makes you think you've got the right to mock her? Quite a few people in this restaurant, if they didn't have better manners, might well point and laugh at *you*, for wearing those shorts and combing your hair into a fringe and holding your knife pencil-grip and drinking a *milkshake* with a *meal*.'

———

I'm not very skilful. I don't know, intellectually, what I'm trying to do. I want it all to be fast and light but to echo, and yet I don't want to be trapped in speed.

———

If I were a man of a pre-feminist generation, with a wife to provide my meals and clean my house and bring up my children, perhaps I would have a free mind for the large thought, the unlimited plan; and free time for night work, for hours without the necessity to think ahead about trivia—will we have veal for dinner or will I send the girls out for Lebanese take-away? Will the dog be lonely all day? Why didn't I defrost the fridge before I went to the market? Or is my mind slack and small for other reasons?

———

Flipped through an old poetry collection. Michael Drayton (who?): 'this ill-fac'd Munky'. I also read again *To Penshurst:* 'The blushing apricot and woolly peach', which for some reason brought up a sob.

———

Oh, frustration and despair, and last week I thought I was getting somewhere. I'm just a middle-level craftswoman. Saw a doco on TV about James Joyce. His vast reading, his intellect, his disorderliness, etc etc. Pooh, pooh, I cry, then the voice-over reads a paragraph from *The Dead* and I'm gasping with tears in my eyes.

———

I feel, when it goes badly, resentful and alarmed at the thought that I must spend the rest of my working life in this discomfort, inadequacy and grief. Grief is not too strong a word for what one feels before one's own weakness and mediocrity.

———

Virginia Woolf in her diary, about trying to write 'the mad scene in Regent's Park. I find I write it by clinging as tight to fact as I can, and write perhaps fifty words a morning…One feels about in a state of misery—indeed I made up my mind one night to abandon the book—and then one touches the hidden spring.'

———

I wish I knew some jolly intellectuals. Well, I do know U. She came over and stayed all arvo. She looked very pretty, with her thick curls well cut. She's lost a lot of weight but when I hugged her I felt the softness of flesh on her torso and realised with pleasure that I am, by comparison, hard and muscular. So I should be, with three aerobics classes a week. She talked endlessly about her husband. 'He was laughing as he played cards and sang along with the radio.' On the beach at night they fought. She hit him. He picked her up and flung her down on her back. 'He tells me terrible things about myself. And I can't help wondering if he's right.'

———

Went to work and fiddled round for half an hour, then began properly to feel it come, and got Athena and Philip into the cafe and the two girls with blood-sucking lipstick walk in, and THEN, oh joy, I swung into the first Poppy-and-Elizabeth scene, also Poppy alone with her school uniform: great, long sentences, one of them at least half a page! Delirious I ran downstairs and bought myself a pastie from the San Remo Bakery.

———

A visitor passed me a joint, also I drank some wine and some pernod and some port. (Only a little of each.) I want to read Freud's *Civilization and its Discontents* but I'm too stoned.

———

Musician: 'Do you ever find that you're working on some piece of art, and all it needs is one final leap to grasp it, but that in order to do it you're going to have to be not a nice person?'

Me: 'Yes. Every day.'

———

Each morning M comes into my room and gels her hair in front of the mirror. I love to watch her preen and skip. Her legs are long and brown in her gingham school dress—she's grown an inch since November. At the Vic Market she took me to see a certain pair of boots: little flat black suede ones, pointy like witches' shoes, that tied at the ankle. She obviously had no hope that I'd buy them. In a rush of generosity I said, 'Try them on.' She did. 'They fit!' she cried in a trembling voice. I bought them with a cheque. She was so excited I thought she'd burst into tears. 'I can't *believe* it!' she kept saying.

———

A big dry wind blew all night from the north. The street has been swept clean, and things have a dry sparkle. The eastern sides of chimneys are sharp and white. The air hisses along our house-side and buffets the small protuberances.

———

I went to work and broke through a brick wall or went round the side of it or dug under it or something: Athena's moral crisis and flight. The pace picked up incredibly. Present tense. A weaving and twining of many a disparate thread. All these years of note-taking, of being what Joan Didion calls 'a lonely, anxious re-arranger of things', are now paying off. I even got in the skier on the colour TV in the Italian cafe! That image has been dogging me for ten years at least.

———

T showed me two drawings of windows, each one with a different weather outside it.

'They're beautiful,' I said.
'Should I put them in the show?'
'I would.'

'But they don't sort of make any social or political comment, do they.'

'For God's sake, woman! They're windows! What more do you want?'

I admired some little dark blue lace-up leather boots K was wearing. He immediately took one off and suggested I try it on. Its slightly damp warmth.

P invited me to come to the framer and see her big pastels: she was showing them to some distant relatives who were interested in buying. The pictures were in a pile on a table, interleaved with tissue paper, waiting to be put into the dusty gold frames she had chosen for them. The ones I saw were striking. I liked them very much. She was asking $650 and I thought that was a fair price. One of the women was so antipathetic I could hardly believe it—an abrasive manner with the subtext 'Nobody makes a monkey out of *me*.' 'You're selling yourself short,' she said harshly, 'by showing us these unframed. I know for a *fact* that there's no point asking my husband to look at things flat out on a table. I know there's no *way* he'd be interested when they're not in frames.' At least a novelist doesn't have to provide decoration for people's new houses.

Will I ring up K and say, 'I like you; I am interested in you'? Or will I do the safe, housewifely thing, that is, nothing?

I will *go to work*.

And after that I went to my office and wrote, without fuss, in an hour and a half, the story the magazine asked me for. It's short, a piece of fluff somewhere between journalism and fiction, but it's nice, it's clean, and I like it. And I know today why people write short stories: because they are *short,* because your imagination can encompass the entire thing all in one go: whereas a novel will hang and hang over you, for a year at a time, like a mountain right behind the house blocking out the sun.

———

Reading Nadine Gordimer's *Selected Stories*. So marvellous, sensible, confident, modest-toned, informative, decent. I can't put it down. I read between putting on one item of clothing and the next. She *knows* a lot. 'She runs a tough line, in her introduction, on writers using other people's lives,' I say to B at Notturno; 'she says of *course* writers have to use other people's lives.' B gives me a wry look: 'Does she?' I take these remarks and glances of hers as reproaches, even warnings.

———

They lowered her coffin into the grave. The rabbi took out a little manila envelope full of fine dirt and sprinkled it over her. Across the heap of clayey soil that had been dug out of the hole lay four or five long-handled shovels and a rake. People (only men) from the watchers approached and took it in turns to scoop up spadefuls of the dirt and throw them in on top of her. When each had done his share he passed on the shovel to the next man, wiped his hands on his trouser thighs and stepped neatly out of the way. One man's pencil fell out of his shirt pocket on to the clay when he bent over to dig. He picked it up quickly, without looking round. They filled the grave right up to the top: they buried her. Put her to sleep. Tucked her into bed and drew the covers up over her—not leaving this last job to strangers. When it was done the rabbi said, 'If you would like to wash your hands, there are several taps over near the gate. Please be careful not to walk on the—please be careful not to walk on the—' He pointed to the sheets of corrugated iron that covered the nearby, freshly dug, empty graves.

At dawn I looked out my bedroom window and saw the dog trotting down the street towards the back gate with a huge knobby bone between her jaws: its knuckle shone white.

I didn't go to work today. But I did *work*. I wrote the account of the Jewish funeral. In other words, I practised. I took notes. I practised. I did not perform.

'He can't stand me when I sob and become abject,' says U. 'I repel him as Jews and homosexuals repel one.' Seeing my jaw drop she adds suavely, 'I know some people would think I was being anti-Semitic, but I'm not.'

The young tram conductor wore an earring that represented a Marmite jar, and several cheap silver rings, one a writhing snake. He did small dead-pan performances from time to time. 'Keep your legs apart,' he said to a woman who was standing near the door, holding a shopping bag between her ankles. '*What?*' she said. 'Keep your legs apart and you'll be able to balance better.' All the women within earshot glanced at each other and laughed. 'I thought for a minute he was going to say something else,' murmured the gap-toothed one beside me. 'Okay, gang, come on,' he called to a group of passengers in a corner. 'I used to say, "Fares please",' he said to his colleague out of the corner of his mouth, 'but that was bloody ridiculous.'

On the Overland to Adelaide I read on in *The Way of All Flesh*. It's quite leisurely, but full of the most shrivelling hatred and bitterness. Dawn. We stopped for a few minutes at Tailem Bend. Now the day is clear, the sky pale blue. The hills are bald and rounded. A triangular dam is so still that I can see the ripples on its floor.

The line swings south and sun bursts into my 'roomette'.

Elizabeth Jolley, in her dutiful way, tried to inform me of the literary status of a woman in an ugly flowered dress and thick pancake make-up to whom she was introducing me. The woman cut across her: 'I've published two novels,' she said, 'and countless stories in the US.' *Countless* was the word she used.

Elizabeth read shyly from a prepared speech full of enjoyable quotations from Tolstoy and Kleist. I love her careful old-fashioned manners. She paused at one point and said into the microphone, 'I'll just have a drink of…this delicious…' She sipped from a plastic glass of mineral water. 'Ah, yes. Lovely.' I wanted to rush up and cast myself at her sandalled feet.

I was astonished when O said to me yesterday in the street, 'I've changed my mind about clothes. I used to think they weren't important and had no meaning, but now I see they're a way of making statements about yourself—even, if I can say it, an attempt to communicate.' This is a huge concession, from a man who once said to me irritably, '*You* make judgments about people based on what *shoes* they're wearing.' (Which is true.)

The married couple argue in their bedroom. Even with the door closed I hear her shout in a rough, angry voice, 'Look! I didn't put *any* bloody Milo in your coffee!' A moment later she passes my room with a histrionic sigh.

When I listen to other writers reading from their work, I sometimes try for a moment to examine, before I give in to it, the way my mind is developing its visual response to the tale. And I realise with a joyful feeling that the same miraculous thing might happen to people who hear me reading from *my* book.

———

After the panel session J and I went, shivering as the day grew cooler, to the piano bar and had some bad coffee and an extraordinary conversation. It went on for at least an hour, and involved what I suppose was me questioning him closely about the way he lives his religion. He had already, in answer to questions by mail, written me an enormous letter, setting it out and also making apologies (as if I'd think he was proselytising) for 'boring' me 'with this stuff'. He talked about wanting to live like Christ, a life of 'submission and humility'. (I'm striking a false note, somehow—like many very important conversations it exists in my memory as a particular kind of mood or emotional state and not as precise dialogue.) He talked a great deal about his father, whom he loves and admires, but also in answer to my awkward questioning about their use of the Bible etc: 'How do you…sort of…organise your approach to it?' 'I go to it for…enlightenment, or information on a particular point, or for entertainment. And I write with a Bible beside me and on top of that a bloody great Concordance.' He told me about the book he's writing, and how it comes from his own childhood. It sounds beautiful, and I think very good, and daring—a cloud stands over the house, and at the end it comes down and fills the house as the boy goes for oil to anoint his father. I was very moved by this story. And I thought again, *I* want to write like that—to have people doing huge things of symbolic meaning.

By the time we left the bar we were blue with cold and shivering. I took his arm and said, feeling shy but that it was necessary, 'I'm really glad we're becoming friends.' 'Oh, so am I!' he said, and tried to put his arm around my shoulders. We were laughing and embarrassed, almost tearful, handicapped by our heavy bags of books, making clumsy movements of affection. He said that when I'd started asking him about Christianity he'd been afraid it would be the end of the friendship: he said he was used to this happening, to being teased and laughed at.

'In the bar,' I said, 'I kept thinking I was going to keel over. I don't know if it's the cold, or if it's a spiritual crisis!'

'Oh, I'm used to it,' he said, making a two-fisted pounding gesture. 'Working out what I think about things.'

As we approached the other writers at the tent we walked more and more slowly.

I said, 'I think there's something huge, and one day it's going to roll over me.'

I don't even know what I meant by that. But I've known it in some secret part of myself for years. As if I have a puny, tenacious little ego, which is straining at holding back a *mighty force*.

I was awake most of the night. At nine in the morning I finally passed out and slept till noon. When I saw J at the tents I felt shy. I didn't know how to follow up the shocking intimacy of the conversation. But he greeted me simply and asked how I was. We sat on the rim of the grassy slope and watched the world go by. An academic I had met once or twice came scrambling up the rise towards us. She said hello to me, and then, while her smile faded, she stared right into J's face and up and down his body, in the most blatantly curious and speculative fashion. It was as if she were raking him with her nails and could not wait to get away and examine them for clues. She moved on and he turned to me. Under the freckles his face had gone white: 'Did you see that?' 'Yep. They'll all be saying we're having an affair. That's how they think.' He dropped his forehead against my shoulder: 'I think that's *rude*. I think that's really *rude*.'

Why do I write down this stuff? Partly for the pleasure of seeing the golden nib roll over the paper as it did when I was ten.

———

Home. My lovely bed. My bright room.

———

I wrote, straight after the scene in the topless bar, a scene between Athena and Dexter in the lobby of a hotel. It made my skin stand up, the cruelty and honour that emerged between them in about a hundred and fifty words.

———

Yesterday F and I went to a lecture by a man who worked with Einstein and is renowned for his ability to explain his theories to laypeople. But it had been advertised in the paper and by the time we got there, five minutes before it was to start, it was so packed that crowds were shoving at each door and people who looked faint were stumbling out gasping, 'I can't stand it in there.' Disappointed, we drove to a swanky bar in Fitzroy and had a cocktail. We were happy. I thought, How lucky I am to be married to this lovely guy!

———

Two people driving at night. On the radio comes a song by Mondo Rock: 'Come, Said the Boy'. One person thinks, 'That song was on last time we drove somewhere together. But I won't mention it, for fear of appearing sentimental.' The other person says, 'This song came on last time.'

———

The day I realised my novel was going to be a short one, and that its domestic subject and setting were quite proper, I walked home from work and passed a print shop, in the window of which stood a copy of that van Gogh painting of the inside of his bedroom: floorboards, a bed, two cane-bottomed chairs, a window. I thought, That's a beautiful painting. And it's only the inside of a room.

Was bound, but now am free.

Two good rousing hymns were sung at the wedding. But why was she marrying this man, who is plainly unworthy of her?

To Paul Crossley's piano masterclass at the Con. After three hours of intense concentration I was completely exhausted. His teaching was very challenging. He was not a giver of praise or even of encouragement, except to one girl who played Ravel; everyone else played Debussy. I loved the language he used: not only because it was clever and striking but because it showed me that the way I have been trying to write about music is not, as I had feared, hopelessly romantic or amateurish. 'A furtive texture,' he said. 'A harmonic wash in the left hand. Then he clears the texture. Let the harmony settle again, before we take off. *Hover* above what you're going to do.' The concept of *phrasing* began to have meaning for me, not to mention *texture*. And now I know what the pedal is for: to 'avoid breaking the sound'.

Paul Fussell, in *Abroad: British Literary Travelling Between the Wars*, quotes Evelyn Waugh: 'Conversation seriously pursued…consists of narrative alternating with "comment".'

A tremendous wind, cold, gritty and in powerful, frightening gusts, blew all day from the north. Then, late in the afternoon a heavy, soaking rain fell. I went to the gym. B was there. She said, 'I'm lonely.' Her face seemed to quiver. I didn't know what to say.

As I approach the end of the novel I can feel it pulling itself into shape, as if I were only a secretary. Never had this experience before—the characters getting the bit between their teeth.

———

B and I saw Robert Meldrum and the magician Doug Tremlett in *The Tempest*. They brought such delicacy, humour and wonder to Prospero and Ariel that I was on the verge of tears. Tremlett, it having been established from the start that Ariel was in bondage to Prospero through gratitude, fear and love, seemed to be holding himself back from evaporating. No chiffon, no light-footedness—he was a solid presence in well-filled white overalls, a turquoise T-shirt and clean runners, his hair cut short with one tiny curved lock on his forehead. He did it all by the extreme slowness of his movements, his density, his powerful focus. His magician's tricks were graceful, breath-taking, yet anything he picked up—a hat, a cane, a scarf—he imbued with a vital importance. What a play! Virginia Woolf's right—Shakespeare is 'incandescent'.

———

And this morning, Sire, I, your handmaiden, *l'umile ancella*, wrote eight pages, and was content.

———

G came in with his pockets sprouting contracts. We talked about good deals; how to be paid what one is worth.

———

The prostitutes are small-mouthed girls who call to a man, 'Wanna girl?' 'No.' 'Sure?' Not many of them about in the morning. I saw a man of twenty-five or so standing at a rubbish bin. His movements, even as he stood still, drew my attention, and when I glanced at him I saw something dreadful in his face: a thuggish thickness in the mouth and jaw, eyes oppressed by a great, dense knot of anguish between the brows. He continually clasped his hands and flicked up his elbows like a boxer loosening up before a fight. He uttered wordless sounds, strangled grunts, as if he were trying to speak but, like Caliban, were only earth.

―――

T wanted to come with B and me to aerobics. From the lobby we could see a man inside the gym doing those repetitive jumps where you keep both hands on the floor. 'Seems a bit *funny*,' said T, 'doing that kind of thing on the *carpet*. Wearing it out.' I shudder with secret pleasure at her criticisms. On our way out afterwards the dopy girl at the desk called to her, 'How'd you go?' 'Oh,' she said grimly, 'okay. I suppose. But I thought it was a bit masochistic.' '*Good!*' cries the girl, beaming.

―――

U commented on 'Postcards from Surfers'. 'Terrific writing. Especially the opening.'

I wonder if one day I'll ever be able to present such a surface that nobody will be able to say '*especially* the…'

―――

At Castlemaine it was very warm. Even the night was milder than I'd expected. Discouraging memories presented themselves as I roved about the slopes picking up firewood. What does this almost-finished book say about men and women? There doesn't seem to be a way of planning this. My attitude emerges as the story tells itself. I couldn't help agonising over it, thinking of the smallness of my scope, the ordinariness of it, its bourgeois nature. What critics will say. What my friends will think and not say. How I will appear before the world. Oh *shut up*.

We stood on a slope and watched the moon rise: up it came, round as a drawing. We saw how the stars became brighter, sat deeper in space. M and her friend struggled to philosophise. They laughed, and were excited. 'I can't sort of *grasp*,' said M, 'what there is *beyond* the universe.' We all played the ukulele when we felt like it. She made up a song called 'In the Paradise Cafe'. The boy read

Tom Sawyer aloud: he couldn't restrain his laughter. I woke at two in the morning, lay there filled with a kind of shame. Looking out at the moonlit bush, silver by night, grey by day. Don't be so proud. Accept criticism, accept editing and guidance. No one will think less of you. I got up at dawn. There were tasks and I did them: finding wood, making a fire, boiling water. The sky became more orange and the wind began to stir. The coming light. It creeps across the dull grass and pinkens it, between the thin trunks. My panic left me. The problem becomes merely the work I still have to do, rather than an indictment of my whole personality and talent and social position.

———

I feel scraggy-haired, thin-cheeked, masculine. At the service station I saw myself drop into a masculine mode: 'talking to a mechanic'. I did not like this but it seemed to happen spontaneously: my hands went into my trouser pockets, my utterances came out sideways in laconic, deprecating half-sentences. I felt like my father.

———

Loneliness without the pleasure of solitude. What will become of us. Awful tension. Shoulders like iron bars. F doesn't like me. Why doesn't he like me? Am I so unlikeable?

———

'Ah well, you can be optimistic and totally without hope. One's basic nature is totally without hope, and yet one's nervous system is made out of optimistic stuff.' —Francis Bacon in *Interviews with Francis Bacon,* David Sylvester

———

T's house is being painted. I love the way she sees colours and shows them to me: the room that looks white until you've been in it for five minutes and then you start to notice that it's grey. The 'teal green' corduroy she's going to make into curtains.

I rewrote the dinner scene, tried to convey the flippancy and darting of their conversation by a careful series of non sequiturs.

―――

An old friend came over for dinner and I was full of dislike for her. She was passive and idle in company, spoke sharply in a 'doesn't suffer fools gladly' manner, offered nothing, and when the meal was over put her booted foot on the corner of the table.

―――

Spectacular dawns I see from my bedroom window. Sometimes I look out at this richness of sky—layer after layer of colour rising from a bed of dove-grey cloud—and I think, This is a rich person's view, or an adult's view. As if I were not entitled to it, or had it only temporarily, or on sufferance.

―――

M comes in from playing hockey with her friend.
  'How did you get home?'
  'We went to Lygon Street and got a free meal at Tiamo, then we—'
  'How did you get a free meal at Tiamo?'
  'We just begged and begged. We said, "Oh, go on—give us one," and they did.'

―――

I typed THE END. I rushed home 'dizzy with unconsumed excitement'. Could not seem to get much of a response from the people present. 'I've finished. I've typed the words THE END.' 'What—again?' 'Guess what, I typed THE END.' 'You'll have more to do.' But then someone went out to get champagne and they made a fuss of me, which embarrassed me, for I felt I should have been mature enough and tactful enough to have demanded less of them. I will never get this right.

Is this 'the artist's' fate? Always to be loved less than I need; or somehow to repel love, or what is seen in the myth or dream of our society as normal marital love? I feel I'm reaching my strength, in my work, but there's a corresponding falling-away...It's terribly sad.

T rang to ask me to go to a film with her. 'It's a twelve-minute short at the festival. It's called *Passionless Moments.* As soon as I saw the title I went to the phone and rang you.'

I'm worried about my clothes: that they will be too informal for Japan. But I've just thought, If I have to put up with 'the artist's loneliness' I will take 'the artist's prerogative', i.e. looking slightly peculiar.

I had never before seen a diplomat go into action. She held a glass in her hand, and smiled, and out of her mouth poured a stream of bland, silly, obvious, trivial clichés, while her face was lit by the same expression of warmth and intelligence that appears on it when she is conversing with her friends.

'And when I got back to Canberra,' said the Japanese professor, 'I found that four out of my five colleagues had divorced and remarried.'
　'Had they married younger women?'
　'Yes. Students. Graduate students.'
　We laughed.
　'Sad, isn't it. Pathetic.'
　'One professor had gone to marriage counselling. The counsellor was a woman. She advised him to get a divorce. Now *they* are married.'

We laughed again, looking away from each other.

I said, 'It's almost immoral.' By then we were both doubled up.

This is what will happen to me. He will leave me and go off with someone younger. In a novel I read by Fumiko Enchi, mention was made of terrible revenges that scorned women wreak on men (spirit possession for example), and of women who 'dissolve their whole beings in the anguish of forgiving men'.

———

'How should I approach Bartok, or Webern, or Schoenberg?'

'Immersion,' says the South African. 'Repetition. But if on a particular day you don't like it, stop listening. That's how I learned.'

———

The huge salesman in the hotel bar mentioned where he came from in an apologetic tone. 'Queens. In Nyork. Have you heard of it?'

'Course I've heard of it! There probably isn't a single place in the USA that I haven't heard of!'

'How about Boise, Idaho?'

'I've seen it written, but never heard it said.'

———

In my dream someone said to me, 'I want to look for some graves.' I said, 'So you can desecrate them?' Even in my sleep I was laughing.

———

I'm starved. Of love.

———

The chief attraction at the reception was a fourteen-year-old wunderkind of the piano in connection with whose name Mozart has been mentioned. He was a pale, soft, neurasthenic creature with feverish eyes set close together, and a lisp. I looked at him with distaste and remembered something Nabokov said about youthful prodigies: 'their sad, pear-shaped bottoms'. He kept rushing up to his guardian (a New York Jewish lawyer who was entertaining me and the diplomat with stories of the young man's successes and talents) and chattering in an oddly child-like way about Maria Callas, whom he ostentatiously admired. After one of his excitable approaches, he dashed away and the lawyer turned to us with an expressive look. The diplomat said, 'Is he always like this?' 'Worse,' said the lawyer. 'He's a pain in the ass.'

———

The diplomat and her daughter were yelling at each other about leotards. The daughter went for the jugular: they were nothing but vanity; the sporting activity is the point; what you looked like while you were doing it was irrelevant. 'That seems to me a rather puritanical position,' I said, dexterously wielding my chopsticks. 'I *like* extreme positions,' shouted the girl. 'I *hate* middle positions.' The wind went out of the mother's sails and she sat there looking at her plate.

———

'What sort of a life did you have in Paris?' asked the old Japanese scholar.

'I was lonely in Paris.'

A smile cracked his severe professorial face. '*Everybody* is lonely in Paris!'

———

Yesterday the diplomat asked me if I'd like to have my hair cut at her hairdresser, 'so you won't have to worry about it.' I politely declined, but I knew she really meant, 'Your hair looks awful.' I remembered the Frenchwoman in Toulouse who put kohl round my eyes, stood back, and said, 'You look *much* better like that.' I can't bear this kind of thing, it makes me feel quite mortified with shame, ugliness and self-consciousness. Like when Whatsername said, with that smile she gets when she's about to be daringly frank, 'I like your hair when it's pushed back at the sides.' I felt like screaming,

'*I* like my hair when it's all shaved off! So get fucked!'

Four groups of firemen in mediaeval-looking costumes walked, one after another, on to the bare, dimly lit stage, and chanted. At first, when I realised that nothing else was going to happen, I imagined that I would soon become bored, but I didn't. The chanting produced a peculiar feeling of being outside time. They did dangerous stunts: one man would shin up a ten-foot bamboo ladder that was held upright by a dozen or more of his colleagues, and would cast himself into impossible positions by twisting his closely trousered legs round the top of the ladder and balancing; then, tapping one palm against the bamboo as if to attract attention, he would extend his torso in a graceful posture. The old woman beside me turned to me in excitement and we laughed together and clapped wildly. People played tiny breathy flutes, a drum, and something I couldn't see in the half-light that sounded like a harmonica but was held perpendicular to the mouth. A great crowd of men, dressed in ordinary trousers, shirts and street shoes, walked slowly on to the stage and made a rhythmic *shh-shh-shhh*, like water squirting. The little flutes wailed above the shh-ing. This went on, crescendo and decrescendo, for what must have been five or ten minutes, but it never occurred to me to look at my watch. Just when I thought I couldn't endure the stillness and the rhythmic sound another second, the musicians began to walk very slowly in a big circle, single file, round the shh-ing men, still playing, and returned to their positions behind. The meaning of all this I could not begin to guess at. At the very end the entire company stood massed in curved rows at an angle to the audience, and the four leaders, older men, sang a song. A very old man, thickset, with an almost shaven grey-stubbled head, was ushered on from the wings and stood in front while the chanting started again. Then one of the four leaders cried out something to the audience and everyone in the theatre clapped their hands—two, three, four, in unison—and shouted out a word, and it was over. Everyone applauded and sprang up smiling and laughing and poured out of the building.

'What did he say at the end?'

'He said, "Now let's all do something together!"'

———

Back in my hotel room I put 100 yen into the TV and saw: a car crash, the dead man's formal headshot; a conference of world leaders, Thatcher, Mitterrand, and Nakasone; two huge guys arm-wrestling; and a modern soap in which a man in a suit hit very hard in the face, knocking her to the floor, a woman dressed in a kimono; this scene occurred in a restaurant—something I cannot *imagine* happening here.

———

A visiting Australian professor lightly suggested that when I give my 'lectures and seminars' I should speak slowly, enunciate clearly, and keep my vocabulary down to about a thousand words. Oh, why did I come? I long to go to Kyoto and stand in a peaceful garden. Do they have gardens in Tokyo? I miss my girl. The schoolgirls here have small waists, slightly bowed legs, rounded cheekbones, thick swinging hair. I ate a delicious breakfast: rice, pickles, miso soup, two slices of cold omelette, and the front half of a dried fish.

———

A long, absorbing documentary at a cinema in Roppongi—old people in a mountain village talking straight to camera about their lives and families, their occupations (charcoal burning; silkworm farming), and *the war*. Many black-and-white still photos, riveting. Their handsome, sober, tender faces, as youths, as soldiers. A man told how his regiment was dumped in New Guinea unarmed and unprovisioned. They buried unripe bananas in the sand. They died of dysentery and malnutrition. He was the only one of his mates who survived. 'I was ashamed to go home. I didn't know where the ship was going. I saw the pine trees. "There are no pines in the tropics. It must be Japan! *Tadaima*!"' An old woman spoke in an artlessly poetic way about a fireworks display in her village, how people came from further down the mountain and sat in her garden to watch. 'And the most beautiful were flags that waved and fluttered as they fell. There were red ones among them.' Gracefully flexing her wrists she swooped her wrinkled hands back and forth in front of her face, down and down and down. A soldier told how his superior officer made him polish boots so much that he had no time to polish his own. '"Stick out your tongue," he said to me. "You can lick them clean." So I did. I licked and licked. *Erghh*. They were covered in dung. But I was a farmer, it wasn't dirty.'

No wonder they lost the war.

———

It's raining. They have laid the garden chairs on their sides in the bar under my window.

———

A bunch of small boys in school hats like inverted pudding bowls was scuffling on the pavement in play. One of them stepped back and accidentally trod on my foot. He turned his face up to me with an almost cringing expression, bowed and said, '*Sumimasen*!'

———

K is very forward with me, but always with the shy person's glossy and frightening barrier of witticisms. He's small and clever and furious. He has bees in his bonnet. He talks a lot, likes talking about himself. An interrupter, an earbasher. I have to push for my share of airtime. I'm not tough enough to fight off his cross-cutting technique. He asks for, and expects in quite a bare-faced way, a great deal of my time: he's lonely, unable to be on his own, demanding, nervous, depressive. He says he likes my work. He says it's 'fabulous'. I can never accept that kind of comment. I just can NOT accept or compute it.

———

I now have two weeks to absolutely *currycomb* the tics and adverbs and adjectives-in-pairs out of this goddamn novel.

———

P lay on her bed and wept. She was grieving over her isolation as an artist. 'I'd like to talk about things with other painters, the men, but they know so much, and I feel sure they'd realise how ignorant I am of all the things they know, and they won't think I'm worth talking to.' This sense of herself as a charlatan or a phoney is something I am all too familiar with. But I don't feel anguished about lack of contact with other writers. I must be more secretive than she is. I hide to work and I have nothing to talk about. Chatting with some smart-arse about semicolons and long sentences is all very well, but it's no more than chat.

———

A man once told me, years after we broke up, that he had built a little shrine inside himself, and that I had got in and kicked it all to bits. At the time I had no idea what he meant. But now I get it, watching another man hovering reverently over the little altar of his sufferings, wanting me to approach and genuflect.

———

Culture Club is in town. Boy George is a plain-looking lad, though journalists go on about how 'pretty' he is. He'll have a double chin in a couple of years, and he has large, white, soft-looking hands, but his voice is gorgeous and there's something good-natured and undramatic about his personality in interviews that makes me like him. He relaxes all the time into a vague cheerfulness, and so does the viewer. When he talks I feel like laughing in a drippy kind of way.

At home we played General Knowledge. F got out his guitar and made up a song about the answer to each question. He was so clever and imaginative, parodying styles and making up rhymes, we were in fits.

―――

We heard about a boy who lit some gunpowder. It exploded and skinned his face.

―――

'He's reading your manuscript. He says it would be better if it had chapters.'

―――

Why married people have affairs: you feel luckier, with a happy secret place in your imagination in which to refresh yourself. My mistake in the past has been to keep it on the front boiler, cooking briskly, instead of turning off the gas and letting it go cold.

―――

I'd like to go to Sydney. Visit my friends. Loll on G's couch in Elizabeth Bay, listen to *La Cathédrale engloutie*, look out the window at the masts, ask him why he wants to get married in a church. Lean on R's cupboard-front in Newtown and watch her dealing quietly with her kids, listen to her light, quick, self-effacing voice, her slight lisp; be near her barely glimpsed and brilliant inner life. Walk in the Botanic Gardens and see the Opera House eggshells shine, water and ships sparkle.

―――

'I've got no friends,' sobbed P.

I roared at her. 'What are you TALKING about? You've got DOZENS! You're just too lazy to go and see them! Look in your fucking address book!'

―――

'This is going to sound very reactionary,' says K, ' but I don't think women should smoke in the street.'

'*I* don't think they should *eat* in the street,' I say. 'I don't think *anyone* should.'

———

F so rarely buys clothes that he can barely bring himself to be polite to shop assistants.

———

But I don't like lying.

———

Some men were loading sheets of building material on to a skip. I walked past and seconds later heard a colossal crash. I ran back. The sheets had toppled and pinned a workman's lower leg against the side of the skip. He was dangling upside down, leg caught, knee bent, head and shoulders and arms resting in crucified position on the pavement. He was uttering strange cries—not harsh, not screams, but light, rhythmic, descending moans, like the sound of someone making love. His Italian workmates were calling out. A shop assistant ran back into the jeans store to call an ambulance. A small crowd gathered. 'Lie 'im down!' called a woman. I walked away.

———

She wrote that my comments on her manuscript were 'like a refreshing breeze blowing into a stuffy room'. How generously people other than me can accept criticism!

———

G called about the book. His voice sounded very close and warm, as if he'd been laughing. 'Hel? I loved it. I laughed, I cried, I shivered, I hugged myself.'

———

It's raining silver and the sky to the east is blazing with a vivid double rainbow, a fatly arched one. Mad spring.

'I used to hit her,' says the man in the bar.

'What sort of hitting?'

'Up against the wall. Backhander across the face. That sort of thing. And it would turn into a fuck. Because there are some women who goad a bloke into violence. It gives them the moral advantage. Years later, after I'd gone away lacerating myself for having been a violent, woman-bashing pig, she came to see me and said, "I wanted to tell you that I see now that I provoked you all those times, that I goaded you into hitting me."'

'Wow. That was honest. How did you feel then?'

'*Furious.* That she hadn't told it to me years earlier, and let me go on punishing myself all that time.'

'Maybe it took her that long to understand it about herself. I think it was big of her.'

He goes silent. Flicks me a complicated look.

M has her school friend over for the night. Together they enter an element quite separate from ordinary life—male and female characters, invented accents, vast fantasies, paroxysms of malicious laughter. There's something terrifying about them.

I love F and I want him to be joyful. I'd like to say to him, 'Let's chuck the whole jigsaw up in the air and see what comes down.' But he wants to hash things over, to make sardonic remarks, to criticise again my horrible personality. The love and attention I have to give him wither on the vine. A line from some forgotten book: 'We always want those we are hurting to be gay.'

A visit from the new parents. She feeds the baby from her enormous breasts, so big she has to lie on her back and lay him belly down across her bosom like a tiny mountaineer.

The Cuban author Guillermo Cabrera Infante says that the writer is important not because he can write but because he can listen. His job is 'to catch the human voice in flight'.

Sex fades, and if one has chosen the right person something else comes to fill the space it leaves. Maybe one day I'll read this over and be overwhelmed with *bitter laughter*.

In the library I sat down with three translations of Rilke's *Duino Elegies*. Translators are a mob of cheats, vain and attention-seeking. An impossible profession. So I stumbled from word to word in the original, without a dictionary. I wanted to groan and weep with frustration. All that knowledge I once had, dissipated through lack of use.

Stranger at the lunch table: 'This is the day after my husband walked out. He came home on my wedding anniversary and said he'd reached a stage in his life where he didn't want the responsibility of a family. I've taken some tranquillisers. That's why I'm not having any wine.' Her elder boy, she said, took to his bed, then asked her, 'What did I do wrong?' The younger boy cried for a quarter of an hour, then came out of his room and said, 'Why don't we all have a game of cards?' Maybe it was the tranquillisers, but something about her calm chilled me. I sat beside her, aware that I was gazing carefully and curiously into her face as she talked. She was very good-looking, with eyes set in deep sockets. 'I'm a pretty tough lady,' she said. 'I'll survive.'

A little girl today at the lolly shop. Seven or so. Silvery blond hair pulled into wispy pigtails. Jeans rolled to the knees, and the most extraordinary legs and feet. Her calves were as developed as a dancer's, slim and with muscles clearly outlined, almost squared. She sprang and leapt about with her sister. She crept after a bird that had hopped under the table looking for crumbs. Something heart-breakingly strong about her legs and high-arched feet.

The mother asked the father to go to the counter for an ice cream. He turned to go, then flung himself back to her with a grimace of discontent and said, '*You* go. I feel an idiot, holding your purse.'

'Marriage *is* a kind of…mystical union,' said the new father. 'You're not only you any more.' Mystical union. I stared at him. The size of the statement, the theological term, dropped casually at the table. I have never, ever felt any such thing, and do not expect to. Like R, I feel that 'in the end, there's only you'.

The newspaper interviewer, young and intelligent and pretty, with a thick plait, seemed disappointed that I was not 'rebellious'. 'Did you have a message?' she asked. 'Were you trying to criticise middle class values?' 'No. I was just trying to tell a story the best way I could.'

Young male photographer: 'Come on. Big smile. Love those big smiles.'

'Please don't tell me to smile.'

'You look starched.'

'I *am* starched. I am a starched *person*.'

Peacocks in the courtyard outside my office window engage in what looks like mating preliminaries: the male puts up his splendiferous tail and strolls about, stretching it forward, curving it over his head, bowing and turning and preening like a Brazilian drag queen. I have a powerful urge to run out there and sink the toe of my boot into his fluffy arse.

———

We rode together into the big park. Spring flowers everywhere—freesias in throngs, and startling growths of kangaroo paw with its dark red, *vividly* red stalks. From an eminence I saw a vast cloud of rain moving in from upriver. It hit us and she fell off her bike—came off slowly and gracefully into a patch of thick grass. It cushioned her. The rain poured down and we were doubled over with laughter. She was too weak from laughing to get up. She knelt there in the undergrowth bowed over with her palms on her thighs.

———

'I burnt all your letters,' he said. 'The postcards exploded. I thought that was significant.'

———

First student: 'That's a cliché.'
　　Second student: 'I put it there on *purpose!* To *disorient* people!'

———

The strange couple arrived late at the dinner party. She paraded in, chin high, teeth blazing. She had skinny little legs and a short dress that barely reached her knees. No sooner had they sat down than she said to her husband, whose little legs were as stumpy as hers were stick-like, 'Dougal, would you go out to the car and get my bag?' He sat still. We all looked at him. 'I won't be able to find it,' he said sulkily. 'Oh, just run out and get it,' she said, as if brushing aside a child's objection. And he did. She spoke with a kind of serene boastfulness: 'One of the reasons why I know more than many people is that we had servants, a butler, a boy—and I read a great deal.' Throughout the meal she was always moulding her husband: 'Dougal. Tuck your serviette into your belt, so you won't keep dropping it and having to hunt for it. *That's* better.' I worked hard for hours, asking questions to keep myself awake. Late in the evening her husband turned to me: 'So. What's s' special about *you*?' I surprised myself by saying calmly, 'Why are you speaking to me like that? I don't know how to answer.' He backed down at once. He said he had taken up golf, and played by himself at the crack of dawn.

Eduard Limonov, in *It's Me, Eddie*, describes a thirty-year-old woman as 'ageing', 'in the autumn of her life'.

Elizabeth Jolley spoke about the huge hotel the Toronto festival had put her in: 'The first night, there was a white flower in the bathroom. The second night, a scarlet flower. Of course this sort of thing is completely wasted on someone of my age.'

'He's a sweet bloke, isn't he.'
'He is. Adorable. But with such vast areas of ignorance! Not knowing what ravioli was!'

I came out of the Arts building this evening after my class and saw a huge, pale-orange moon rising out of the Swan River. It was so big that for a moment I didn't know what it was. And then I wanted to shout to people passing, 'Why aren't we all standing still gazing at it? Or down on our knees praying to it?'

She had long smooth dark hair drawn back off her ears and temples by two combs, and skin that at first I thought was made-up; as the evening progressed and we struck up conversation, she came and sat beside me and I saw that her skin was bare, and quite perfect.

I liked her. She was extremely slim, and was wearing a cobalt blue jumper with shoulder pads. Once, in an absent moment, she pushed her left sleeve up past her elbow. This gesture made her seem less perfectly presented; it was the moment at which her beauty ceased to repel me. I looked happily at her lovely face while she talked.

———

'Some people are Christians,' said J, 'some people are atheists or agnostics, and some people agonise about it. They're sub-Christians. I think that's what *you* are.'

———

The house: an uncertainty of taste, a bit too cluttered, furniture not quite the right shape for the room that contains it; but pleasant, light and clean. If I owned a house I would always be getting rid of things.

———

Homosexual man ten years older than I am: 'My parents always took care to teach us that we mustn't show our emotions—that they are tedious, and a bore and a nuisance to other people. I learned this lesson so well that as an adult I have found myself in a situation where someone will leave me because he thinks I don't need him.'

———

At dinner the surgeon asked me why I write with a pen rather than using a dictaphone or a word processor. 'Why would I?' 'Because it's faster and more efficient.' 'But it's my life's work. I'm not in a hurry.' I was surprised to hear myself make that answer.

———

When I play the piano I have a lot of noble and generous thoughts. Moral thoughts. Correctives to what I actually *do*. In my life I have gone round hurting people. I would like to ask everyone I know: On what basis do you make moral decisions? I know what they'd say: 'You've always been good at getting what you want.' But now

I can't, and I don't like it.

A dream about a heap of old fans that I found on the floor behind a couch. They were all made of ivory and clearly of value. I picked them up, one by one. They were heavy, smooth and very beautiful. One of them consisted of so many slats that I couldn't open it right out: as if it were a full circle of slats, and not in a fan form at all—I could not handle its richness. Another had too few slats, only two or three, and even those were so loosely connected that they flopped in the hand, like keys on a ring.

'What could a fan represent?' I asked my hostess.

She looked slightly panicky: 'Fresh air?'

The only passionate love that can co-exist with civilised daily working life is the love we have for our children. The other sort either loses its madness and becomes something else, or blows everything sky-high.

I opened the front door. It was the professor. He handed me the cheque for the week's work, and said without preliminary, 'What's speed?' His son had rung him from Sydney, asking for money 'for a ticket home'. He showed me a photo of a gaunt, good-looking boy of twenty or so, dressed in fashionable rags, his hair with that gelled, torn-out-by-the-roots look. Thank God for Javo. My girl sees no romance in *that*.

'I should tell you I've read your book in proof,' said the visiting writer. 'Brendan had it at his place. He was sure you wouldn't mind.' He added, in a light, dismissing tone, 'I rather enjoyed it.'

Is that *all* you feel about it? Is that *really* all?

With the drawing pens K gave me I begin to understand the limitations of the rapidograph: so rigid, the line unvarying. With the dip pen you get thick and thin, and curlicues, and the way you can draw a striped jumper is absolutely *voluptuous*.

―――

The new parents were moving house and I went to give them a hand. I helped them carry boxes and cartons for an hour or so. Eventually I said, 'Well, I'm off now.' He looked at me with an expression I couldn't read. His face was white, even strained. 'You were mad to come,' he said. 'Dunno why you stayed so long.' I cried on the way home.

―――

'Did you get my letters?'

'Yes. It's the problem of timing. When I needed the letters they didn't come, and when they came I didn't need them.'

―――

In the roadhouse the food was what you'd expect and I loved it. I ordered a nut sundae. 'What flavour topping?' asked the lacklustre waitress. 'Chocolate,' I whispered, flooded with bliss.

―――

I'd go outside except that a large Alsatian is loose in the motel compound, roaming about in that smooth, low-backed way they have; I heard deep barking first, then looked out and saw the dog, posing like a dingo against the swimming-pool fence, favouring one hind leg and dragging its lead.

―――

One of Elizabeth Jolley's stories starts: 'Every small town has some kind of blessing.' And so does every blighted motel. The tiny room, the sagging bed, but when I climbed up and cranked open the bathroom window, what I saw was a sunny morning and a big paddock full of what I ignorantly imagined was wheat. Something yellow.

Rereading my letter I saw I had smudged the ink while turning a page, at such a point that he'd think it was the blot of a tear. Oh *no*. I threw it in the bin.

'If I asked you now to drop everything and run away with me,' said K, 'you wouldn't, would you.'
 (*Hangs her head*) 'No. But I would've. Once.'
 'What changed?'
 'I started thinking.'

Peter Handke's notebooks, *The Weight of the World*. Intense pleasure at the tininess of his observations. Actually, they're not observations so much as junctions between moments. When I read them I feel that I am not after all crazy or even weird. I feel strengthened, *private*, encouraged. I feel the worth of very small things. The whole cast of his mind is familiar to me.

Indira Gandhi has been assassinated.
 'They got her and missed Maggie,' said F.
 'Only just.'
 'She'd finished cleaning her teeth only a few moments before.'
 'It's because those idiots mess around with bombs,' I said. 'Guns are more accurate.'
 As if we were professionals, or had considered such actions ourselves.

P wheeled her bike towards me across the grass. Her shirt was the colour of the grass, her bike basket that of the daisies. It was spring.

When people have been drinking they taste of wood.

A young man sings tunefully and wordlessly in the street: 'dada–*da* da–*da*dada*da*.' Writing those sounds, a blast of memory—being taught to write. At Manifold Heights State School. A flash of the old building. The objective correlative is the loop loop loop action of dadadadadadada.

I love to make F laugh. How handsome he looks when his face is filled with teeth.

'"I want you to go on living for many years." I was glad to hear her say that. It was a bright, pure, friendly night, reasonable through and through.' —Peter Handke, *The Weight of the World*

'*Faut pas contrarier les fous.*' In French cartoons a mad person is drawn with a funnel as a hat.

'Do you think there's anyone in the world who doesn't like Bach?'

He shrugs, fills his cup with strong tea. 'I don't know. It'd be like not liking water.'

When the English teacher got a posting to Inner Mongolia she took a whole suitcase full of sanitary pads and tampons—'They stuff themselves with rags, or, out in the country, leaves'—but her menopause came, and she's never had a period since.

'Writing: safe again.' —Peter Handke. He's more brutal with himself than I have ever been. He inspires me to try to be more truthful in this book. It's hard, for I am always hiding something, either from myself or from the person who may or may not, today or on some future day, read this and be inclined to think less of me.

K calls from some hotel, to tell me, thick-voiced from crying, that his friend, whom I didn't know, has killed himself. With pills. 'He set it up. He told his girlfriend to go away for the weekend, said he was going to work; didn't turn up at work but when people went to his place there was no answer and his car wasn't there. After a couple of days they broke in. They found his little body in there.' He was crying; so was I. 'He wasn't a close friend of mine. But he was one of the pure ones. He wasn't one of the guilty ones. It's the dirty, gritty ones who survive.'

Next day he calls to tell me he's bought me a couple of Exacto cotton jumpers.

HG: (*thinks*) I *hate* Exacto jumpers and they are *not cotton*. (*says*) 'That'll be a nice surprise—thanks.'

I make myself *sick*.

The gardener tells me I must see Sissinghurst before I die.

I ask, 'Why aren't Australian gardens as wonderful?'

'Because we don't believe in straight lines.'

Handke: 'I thought of art as a parachute that would stop me from falling.'

Last night I turned out the light and lay on my bed. Warm night. I was awake. I remember now that I said out loud, 'People need to be loved.' I found that my hands were near each other, and clasped them. Then I said the Lord's Prayer, very slowly, not sure after each line that I would remember the next. And when I got to the end I felt better, so I went back to the beginning and said it again. I tried to think, with each phrase, of its practical application to my life.

'Forgive us our trespasses, as we forgive those who trespass against us.' I thought of F, of my anger and harshness. I thought it would be better to be firm, and not to try to save myself by hatred. This morning, having remembered the prayer, I feel as if I've stumbled on something useful. A technique.

———

K was walking in front of me along a narrow, overgrown track between two rows of graves. I said to his back, 'Sometimes I think I might become a Christian.'

His face appears, over his right shoulder, in a slow, firm, dramatic movement. He keeps walking, still looking back at me. His look, how can I describe it? Partly for comic effect, as if to say, 'Oh, come off it.' But also a flash of incredulity that his sophistication cannot quite conceal.

I laugh: 'You bit.' Protecting my flank, instantly.

People don't respect each other's serious dilemmas as much as they respect, for example, each other's tastes in food.

———

Morning, at the bathroom mirror. 'How did I get such a good-looking daughter? And I so plain.' 'He-*lern*.' (Carefully combing her wet fringe into one eye.)

———

I feel I've been dragged into secrecy, and I hate it, I never wanted to, I think it's wrong and it makes me terribly unhappy. I dread *bitterness*. I must be careful of my *tone*. And not to speak as if all pain should now END instantly.

———

When people came to look at the suicide's body, his sister said, 'Doesn't he know he'll have to go through it all over again?' Belief in reincarnation as a deterrent to suicide.

———

The GP told me I was too thin. She said to drink milkshakes or I would get wrinkled. I said, 'I am already.'

My sister's elegant dress and grey boots, her intelligent, rapid gathering together of points and insights about Dad: '*That* must be why he keeps buying new houses and shifting Mum around—he doesn't want her to stay anywhere long enough to develop friendships that might exclude *him*. His mother died. All his daughters have grown up and gone. He lost his sister—' We stared at each other in horror as she fitted the pieces together.

A letter from a friend. '*Dear* Helen,' he writes. Surely if *he* likes me I can't be such a monster.

On the way to the cinema T said, 'I must get some petrol.' After the movie, which we hated and walked out of early, we set off up the Nepean Highway. I remembered her remark about the petrol but, fearing to be thought bossy, said nothing. Halfway up the St Kilda hill we ran out. We crossed the road to a hamburger shop to ask where the nearest petrol station was. We *had a hamburger*. It was early evening, still light. The Greek woman squeezed lemon juice on to the meat. Our food was delicious. We carried the jerry can up the hill to the petrol station, eating as we walked and talking happily. We filled the can, took it back to the car, did the necessary and drove calmly home.

I answered J's letter. 'Something is "travelling furiously towards me". I don't think it's God. It's some sort of force, and it's inside me, and I've been feeling it coming for a year or more, and now I feel its *might*, and it's a force of immense good, and it will connect me with the oneness of things, it's coming through my dreams, and what I'm having to do is clear the decks so that it can be unobstructed.' And he replied, patiently, 'It hurts to be quickened.'

I feel I'm fighting for my life. Walking down Rathdowne Street to collect a mended shoe I have a large, painful lump in my throat. I'm engaged in some colossal moral struggle. Am I trying to bargain with God? That is not good enough. I try to think of someone wise I can go and talk to. Names occur but none of them will do. I'm aching all over, all the time. Bleeding too. Muscles like rocks. Fallopian tubes in pain. Left thumb joint swollen and sore. I was so unhappy, yesterday, that I thought, Maybe I'm the sort of person who will go mad. Things I looked at had no meaning. The sky was dull with clouds.

It is perhaps always hard to find a person who will play out a drama with you right to the end, and not stroll off the stage before the killing starts.

'When I get garrulous in restaurants,' carolled U, 'my daughters get more and more remote and aristocratic.'

School holidays and M comes down with a bad cold. I put her into my bed and 'tickle her face with a particularly nice feather' until she falls asleep. Then I lie down beside her and read Jung until I fall asleep too, at which point the phone begins to ring.

K says he feels 'glum' that it's over. And I'd been thinking of broken hearts and madness!

F and M played a card game last night of such ferocious competitiveness that it made me nervous to be in the same room. I liked being with them, though: they were on the bed and I was at the table writing letters, and on the cassette player was a tape of gospel music from a radio show. Room full of light and noise and laughter and cries of outrage from the card game, while I was permitted to be present and yet absent. Between songs the singer gave a mild little account of himself: 'I believe in Jesus. I'm really into it, actually.' The card players looked up with grimaces, but I kept on listening. On the bottom of a letter I wrote, 'Do you believe in God, Herbert?' It could be a terrific opening scene in a movie. A lot is happening.

---

5 am. The air is pink and the moon is squashed and pale. A small, steady breeze is running smoothly up the street from the east.

I thought my head was going to burst, I felt so interrogated and observed. Bashed my head against the wall. He cried and tore his hair, hit his forehead with his palms.

At the wedding I saw a row of people snigger when the vicar earnestly invited Jesus to come into the new couple's home, and to stay. Then the passage from Corinthians about *what love is*. How wonderful—but secretly I bet that they're thinking of it as a tribute to their own romantic and sexual infatuation.

I dreamt that I went back to our old house and found that a beautiful archway had been constructed, a high, curved, classical one, halfway down the short path to the front gate. Its purpose was to bear climbing roses, of which only the strong twisted stems were already there—no leaves or flowers.

One of life's great pleasures: using my pen when I have just put a new nib in it.

On the beach a beautiful Weimaraner had found a dead bird and was tearing it apart, spitting out mouthfuls of feathers. We bought mediocre fish and chips in Fitzroy Street and ate them shuddering in the doorway of a closed shop.

'What's the matter?' says M.
   'Hopeless love.'
   'Oh, you talk like a book. Which one of them do you prefer?'
   'It's not that simple.'
   'Yes, but which one *do* you?'
   'Really it's not that *simple*.'
   'It's just *silly*. It's like one of those love comics I've been reading.'

The old Vietnamese man was full of anti-Communist bitterness. He said that before the French came Vietnamese society had no classes. I found this hard to believe, especially when he then began to speak of kings, princes and dukes.

There they sat in the cafe, two tall fair blessed ones, at a table halfway back, drinking mineral water. They showed me their jewellery: her rings, one with a diamond; his Russian one, three rings entwined; her pearl ear-studs, his black and gold watch, her black pearl double-strand necklace. I found this naïve display piercing to the heart and tear-ducts. But then they spoke disobligingly of someone I'm fond of, and lost my sympathy.

1985

'Have you been in my room?'

'No. Downstairs.

'Listening to us fighting?'

'Yes.'

'Where were you?'

'Under the stairs, near the telephone.'

'Did you hear everything?'

'Yes.'

(*Hand over mouth*) 'Was I awful?'

She laughs slyly.

The two bodies found in the tray of a ute. Decomposing corpses. The girl. I knew her. I can grasp this fact intellectually but in no other way.

'People who've had something dreadful happen to their children seem to have a glass wall around them,' said U. 'Ordinary people can never really contact them again.'

I sat down and made a list of people I knew, of my age or younger, who had died. There were fifteen. And I'm only forty-two.

———

Sergei Bondarchuk's *War and Peace* on SBS. How Tolstoy does those moments where a character for a split second gets everything wrong: Prince Andrei, waiting outside the bedroom while his wife is in labour, hears a baby cry and says, 'Why on earth have they brought a baby in here?' And when he's lying wounded after the battle of Borodino and sees the man next to him having his leg amputated, hears him sobbing, then recognises him as Kuragin, the man he hates who tried to elope with Natasha: 'Oh, why does *he* have to turn up here?' Crying over all this I kept thinking of the two kids in the ute, the bludgeoning and shooting. Their funeral tomorrow.

———

'Usually,' said the priest beside the two flower-loaded coffins, 'I wear white vestments at a funeral, when the person who's died was old. Today I almost decided not to vest at all.' His voice was trembling. 'But then I decided to wear red. Red is a vibrant colour. And it's the colour of martyrdom.'

———

How the men carried the coffins: each locked his free arm round the next one's waist—a gesture of tender, manly comradeliness.

———

At the wake the murdered girl's stepfather stood with his friends. We were telling old stories, making each other laugh. Once he put his hand over his face and wept silently; tears poured down his cheeks. I kept my arm around him. After a moment he took his hand away and resumed his part in the conversation.

———

I read through the first draft of my story and saw immediately the point at which it goes off the rails. It gave me great satisfaction to know that my critical apparatus is in working order.

———

When I've written something strong that's on the right track I have an urge to get up from the table. I leave the room, walk to the shop, have a coffee. And when I come back, confident that I've got something solid to build on, I reread the last phrase and find it *better than I had remembered*.

I called P in Paris, and heard $29.30 worth of information about her vaginal infection.

I read a short piece in French by Roland Barthes, about how he guessed Proust had changed his thinking and his behaviour in order to write *À la Recherche*. Now I understand why people love Barthes. His tone is friendly, he is quite at ease with the simple, he says things that many another would have considered beneath his notice because someone else would already have thought them. He is really tackling the subject, not trying to impress anyone. Completely charming, direct and comradely with the reader.

I still have a 'secret life' in my mind. But who doesn't? And it only troubles me when I'm in a mood to trouble myself. I'll use anything that's available at such times.

Bushfires. Three people burnt to death at Kilmore. One of those mouth-of-hell days, air that dried the skin in seconds, north wind. The light an ugly dull yellow. When we sat in the garden to eat our dinner the wind dropped and a coolness came. But flakes of ash fell from the sky and gathered on our clothes and our plates.

Saw two Truffaut movies: *La Peau douce* and *Baisers volés*. One thing he's really good at is the tiny encounter with the nutcase. The student ex-friend who runs into Doinel on a flight of steps and tells him a string of obvious lies about a TV channel having accepted his scripts. The stranger in the cream raincoat who approaches the heroine, declares his love for her and his determination to devote the rest of his life to being in her company, then walks away, saying over his shoulder, '*Je suis très heureux.*' The girl says to Doinel, '*Il est complètement fou, ce type-là.*' This is the last line of dialogue in the movie. *Wah.*

It's ten years since I heard from him but now he calls from Sydney to tell me his mother's got pancreatic cancer. A year to live. When she opened the door to me she looked very small, and younger, as if her face, which I had never before seen without pancake make-up, had softened and lost its social mask. We stood with our arms round each other and she cried. She took me into the bedroom and sat me on the bed and began to talk very rapidly about some baby clothes she'd bought at a sale, years ago, and stashed for the birth of grandchildren. She wanted her son to know where they were, for later. 'We've loved each other for a long time, haven't we,' she said. Surprised, I realised that I had loved her much less than she had me; that I must represent something about her son's past that she did not want to lose. That night she was in my dream. She burrowed her head under my clothes and began to suck on my breasts, one after the other.

At the Carlton Baths B and I saw an African man set upon by some horrible very young teenage girls from the flats. We were frightened of them.

On the grassy area their group, scarcely out of puberty, emitted a disturbing erotic vibe. He must have made the mistake of speaking to them flirtatiously. He asked them for a drink. They laughed, and cursed him. He said, in his slow English, 'Are you not even a little bit kind?' They walked on his leg, poured cordial on his body, stole his watch, cigarettes, shirt. Throughout their attack he never raised his voice, and this was his only remaining scrap of power.

'Girls are worse than boys,' B remarked on our way home. 'You feel there's no end to their cruelty and malice.'

One thing I know I will never receive due credit for, EVER, and that is the amount of cleaning I do in this house. I am the *only one* who ever cleans the lavatories. Sweeps the stairs. Scrapes food dribbles off the cupboard doors. I clean the bathroom basin every other day. I sweep the kitchen, I sweep the yard, I defrost the fridge, I iron the tablecloths, I tidy the benches, I put away the newspapers. I do this work, mostly, without thinking. But when F tells me he works harder than I do, the household jobs come to my mind with *force*.

The old writer lives alone in a high, airy apartment with pretty furniture and a cheerful orderliness. She says that married people have affairs *only* to hurt the other. She says that spouses are jealous of writers, artists etc because we have this area to function in where they can't go, and where they can't hurt us or punish us, i.e. where we are free.

Three jolly plumbers came and fixed the blocked toilet. In the backyard a minor but sudden unblocking sprayed one of them with shit. Until he laughed we didn't dare to. He shook himself and hopped around on one foot, flapping his hands. His teeth were very white, his eyes bright blue.

'What a hot night!'
   'It's not a very hot night. I don't feel much heat.'
   'I didn't say "very hot". I just said "hot".'

'To me a hot night is over thirty degrees. I'm even going to put my doona over me.'

———

It seems I am a really awful person. Pushy, aggressive, demanding, always wanting everything to be clear, worked out, resolved. Also I have bad table manners: I was the first to put out my chopsticks at Brilliant's when the food was served. My enthusiasms, my expectation that others will follow me, lead people to do so against their will: apparently I phrase suggestions in a way that brooks no refusal. When I said 'Let's go to the nude beach on Sunday', my manner made him say, 'All right' instead of what he really felt which was 'Maybe'. Growing more pathetic, dismal and contemptible every minute, I tried to explain my feeling that there is a link between my 'enthusiasms' and the bluff that's needed to be a writer. No, no—many writers are quite introverted. I will have to tone myself down. I couldn't help crying. Silent sobs, with a lot of tears running out. I despised myself for giving way to a spasm of self-pity. I wish I could bawl out loud, get some voice into it and *howl*.

———

I have read in feminist literature about women who could not handle their own talent: who were ashamed of it, or tried to hide it. I never thought I would become one of those. But one comes under certain subtle pressures that are unforeseeable in their form, direction and detail.

———

I dreamt I went to a party in a garden. Bikies were there. I left my old green shoulder bag in an unattended room and when I went back to find it, it had gone. I was scared of the bikies who looked as if they might turn nasty, so I didn't complain about the bag, but moved quietly round the party on my own, looking for it in every conceivable place, without luck.

I made some curtains for my room and they are a disaster.

The women talked about 'spiritual' things and how sad it is that our husbands are afraid of them, or scornful, and cannot share them.

The prisoners in the film about Uruguay, when guards were present, were obliged to stand with their heads bowed. Lined up against the cyclone wire fence they looked, from a distance, like a row of hanged men.

I watched Q, the dressmaker, waiting at the cash register to buy a big slice of watermelon. I saw the graceful angle of her leg and I thought, She's beautiful and full of grace; she likes me; she does not defer to me, nor does she need to undermine me; she has a private mind and a private life; we are not in competition; her areas of competence are so different from mine that we never clash. I envy—or rather *intend to be*, one day—a woman like her. Or those older women writers I've met, who at sixty live alone in a lovely flat, work calmly and with recognition, *have friends*.

Bumped my head hard on the window frame. Wanted to cry; gave a few sobs and gasps, sitting at my table; but realised, as I heard myself beginning, that I *must not*; because I have a day of social duty ahead and must hold it together. I was also shocked and alarmed, even as I controlled myself, by the immensity of sadness that I need to cry about: like glimpsing a grey ocean. I quickly closed my eyes. I sat there with my hands over my face and my elbows on the table and thought, I am desperate. At the same time I thought, And I must write this down. Virginia Woolf and Guy de Maupassant on this subject. What sort of a creature am I?

Damp sand. Flat water, pale silky grey with tints of mauve and pink if one looked very carefully. Hundreds of seagulls circled above the beach. I noticed many moth-like insects in the air and tried to see if they were being hunted by the birds. The life of a wild animal: the basic element must be HUNGER. How many small moths would it take to fill a seagull's stomach?

F says we are 'like adolescents'. He tilts back his head and howls like a dog at the moon: '*Oooooooooooooooo*.' I can't help laughing.

Days of bitter fighting. Sometimes we seem to get somewhere, and emerge sobered, chastened. Then we treat each other with quiet respect. At these times I feel like a human being again, instead of a very bad and wrong person, a sack of different sadnesses being hauled around by a skeleton.

In Emma Jung's essays, *Animus and Anima*, I find that the animus presents itself in many guises, and that one of these is 'a pseudo-hero who fascinates by a mixture of intellectual brilliance and moral irresponsibility'. Surely this is a description of the character called Philip who keeps turning up in everything I write.

F's workmate brought his girlfriend to dinner and we had a wonderful time. She is a young woman who manifests the opposite of what is meant by the phrase 'full of shit'. She was wearing a little green hat in a wartime style, soft material made into a turban. I watched her dancing with him to a Billie Holiday record: that clear blankness of concentration that comes over a dancing woman's face, the readiness to respond in a formal way to whatever might be asked of her legs and torso. The hem of her green crepe dress was down and I sewed it up for her. She kissed my cheek by way of thanks.

The teenage girls, going out to Johnny's Green Room in their clever, bright, improvised clothes: scarves artfully tied, an orange suit from the sixties, a battered golden bag. So fresh and pretty. Full of hope. Their eyes were shining. Not children any more, but only just starting to be adults.

At the dinner we drank tequila and exchanged tales of weak people enabled by fury to stand up against tough ones. A man had made three big teenagers clean up a kids' playground he had come upon them smashing. A woman saw a kid walking down the street carrying an axe. 'Every time he passed a tree he chopped a big chunk out of it. So I went up to him and shouted, "You do that once more and you'll get that axe in your *head*."' 'What did he do?' She shrugged. 'Ran home.'

A woman in Brisbane reviews *The Children's Bach*: apparently it is 'written with great cynicism towards human nature—a more unlovable bunch of characters would be hard to find'.

I see that compared with Doris Lessing I am lazy and a spendthrift.

The sick woman, in her retirement village, talked without stopping for hours. I made myself stay three, then four. I thought, Go the extra mile. You are healthy and young. She is lonely and sick, and she needs you. The cancer management man, she said, had asked her if she could remember any shock in her life, any grief or anger. She told him she'd always been angry about 'what men do to women'; and then she remembered to mention that twenty years ago her daughter had been murdered.

In the cafe this morning a grey-haired old man came in, wearing a fawn safari jacket and shirt, polished brown shoes and socks, and no trousers. As he walked you could see his red underpants flash in the vent of his jacket. The Italian waiters accepted this strange fellow with an impressive nonchalance. He went to the toilet and back, sat at his table, and was brought his coffee just like everyone else.

———

I feel great relief that I did not conduct my side of the thing secretly. I did my cleaning-up and straightening as I went along, like a brutal sort of housework; but on his side K let the dirt accumulate, and now the rotting things and dried chop bones are being found behind the piano. 'It was always easier for me than it was for you,' he said. Yes, because he lied. But the law of karma is reasserting itself. 'Want some advice?' I said. 'Stay off the piss. You won't want to be handling this kind of thing with a hangover. And drunk people say things they regret later.'

———

TV interview with the Aboriginal girl who is Penthouse Pet of the Year.
 'You must be very excited. Did you get much sleep last night?'
 'No. I was awake half the night looking at my diamond watch!' She holds it out to the camera. 'It cost four and a half thousand dollars!'
 Her eagerness, her naïve pleasure in the $80,000 worth of prizes and rewards, cuts no ice with the disapproving woman interviewer, who proceeds to guilt-trip her about feminism and her Aboriginal blood and responsibilities.

———

The surrogate mother was asked on TV how she had arrived at the price she charged her couple. 'Well, I asked myself how much

I could earn if I was fully employed for nine months, and I worked it out at $6000.' The paltriness of this sum was not remarked upon. 'And if you did it again, how much would you charge?' She thinks, then gives a daring little smile and a sideways glance. 'Ooh…I'd charge…ten thousand?'

'What about labour?' said T crossly. 'Surely that'd be overtime?'

———

Sunset last night was like a swap card I once had of a pirate ship: torn clouds, dramatic perspective, orange, gold and green. And now a dawn sky of delicate purity, and a smell of eucalypts. Maybe a marriage can get up again and walk, after a terrible beating.

———

'What've *you* been up to?'

'Nothing I wouldn't talk about if the right person asked me in the right tone of voice.'

———

'It is when one's talent has been recognised that the great misery of the creator begins.' —Camus

———

I met Raymond Carver in Sydney and he signed a copy of *Will You Please Be Quiet, Please* and gave it to me. I wanted to tell him how much his work has meant to me but there was only time to shake hands.

———

In the street, noticing that as usual B was dragging two paces behind me and to one side, I slowed down, again and again, to see if it was *me* doing it; but no, each time she slowed down as well, so I was always in front, no matter how I tried to walk beside her.

'You mean,' said the Jungian, 'that if you put down the reins she doesn't pick them up—they just lie there?'

———

Someone got into the Adelaide zoo and slaughtered sixty animals. Stabbed them, cut their throats, sliced out their entrails.

―――

Went to *Die Walküre* last night. I loved the way a character would sing a very long *story*.

―――

The French tutor said she had been very anxious before the surgery; that it was hard to submit to the fact that she was obliged to put total faith in the anaesthetist (she could not pronounce the word, and made a gesture of poking something into the back of her hand). 'But,' she said, 'when I thought that otherwise I might die, I found it easier to…get more philosophical.' At these three words, so characteristic of my serious, thoughtful teacher, I was moved, and grabbed her hand. She said that since the operation she has been less bothered by the small anxieties of ordinary life.

―――

The dreams: so dense.

―――

For twenty-four hours I had nausea and diarrhea. It was a hot autumn day with a dry wind pouring in through the window. M looked after me nobly, without signs of revulsion, even when she came in and found me on my hands and knees over a bowl on the bedroom floor, spewing bile. It was Palm Sunday. They say there were 120,000 people at the anti-nuclear rally. I read some Jung, some of *The Waiting Years* by Fumiko Enchi, bits of *A Passage to India* and stories from David Malouf's *Antipodes*.

―――

Dreamt that in a house on stilts, above water, I was laid up and then found I was ill and soon to die. I looked at objects with regret and longing. I was lifted by people not quite strong enough and dumped on to a stretcher.

I wish I could get this tone, and pace, in fiction.

―――

A 'bloodless coup' in the Sudan. The president goes to Washington, and as soon as his back's turned nine army officers take over. He ends up stranded in Cairo.

'Imagine,' says F. 'He can't go back. All his things…'

―――

Last night, Greek Good Friday, a thousand people passed under my bedroom window in the almost-dark, each one holding a burning candle. I leaned out to watch them. Our street was packed to the gutters with slowly stepping, murmuring Greeks, whole families, a bearded patriarch. A mass of flowers, like a huge cake, was borne along by a group of four. A brass band quietly played a hymn I remembered from school. No one was singing but as I watched the stream flow by, the words of the hymn came back to me: 'casting down their golden crowns around a glassy sea'.

―――

In the Fitzroy Gardens I made it clear to K. 'It's like carrying a wardrobe. We have to put it down and walk away.' We stood in the middle of the huge lawn with our arms round each other. He stepped back. I saw that his glasses were fogged up. 'Sorry about that,' he said.

―――

'Why don't you *like* me?'

'What *is* this question? Why do you ask this question?'

'What do I *do*, that makes you not like me?'

'You're *there*. That's all.'

On my way home I bought a 'couple self-help' book at Readings and ripped through it greedily. It suggests very practical ways of breaking destructive patterns of behaviour. I cried over it because its examples were so petty, so familiar, and so utterly convincing.

'My husband and I have agreed to part,' said the woman in the post office to her friend. 'My presence is inhibiting his creative development.'

She said this without irony or apparent animus.

———

I held their Airedale puppy in my lap. I tickled it and it groaned.

———

A young girl was found dead, naked except for a pair of underpants, in a St Kilda gutter. Dumped there after she had overdosed. What savagery. To leave your friend in a cold gutter without even covering her—not a sheet, a rug, an old coat.

———

In the bookshop I picked up the new *Oxford Anthology of Australian Literature*, a book whose existence was unknown to me. I knew I could not be represented in it because they would have had to ask my permission. I examined its index. No, I wasn't there. I felt the world seesaw. I walked to the tram stop wretched. I am full of shit. I am crude, a beginner. People must laugh at me behind my back. I posture as a writer and at forty-two I can't even get into the Oxford book.

———

He seems to be full of anger towards me. The slightest misstep on my part brings out a jet of it.

———

A couple passed us on the beach. We guessed they had met through a dating agency. I said the man couldn't find a woman because he talked all the time and expected her to listen. F said the woman couldn't find a man because she listened all the time with her head on one side and made attention-murmurs, and was 'limp'.

———

'The deeper you go,' said the Jungian, 'the more sceptical you must become.'

———

B was so sick of me that when she saw my writing on the envelope she tore it up unopened and threw it away. Later, she learned it had contained a publisher's cheque for several hundred dollars, for a job we did together. She had to call me and eat crow.

———

I'm so tired, even after all that sleep. My head and body are full of lead.

———

In the Exhibition Gardens I saw a man walking with a bitch and her pup at his heels. The bitch ran smoothly, smiling, but the pup kept stumbling and tumbling in his eagerness to keep up. He rolled right on to his back in the dry plane leaves, scrambled to his feet and galloped on.

———

J and I walked in the cemetery with the dog. A grey afternoon. He felt the cold. Sometimes we walked with our arms around each other. He said I was skinny. He said he had lost a stone. I think he was still in shock from the media attention he got in Sydney for the big prize. He spoke rapidly, almost gasping. I saw that my job was to give him my full attention, to ask questions and listen to the answers. I asked him if his ego was swollen. No, he said, the opposite: he felt he was small, he was nothing. He told me about his church, how it 'goes back to the time before there was a pope'.

———

The way M answers the phone: with a rising intonation, a little breathless—'Hello?'—as if to say, 'I'm ready for whatever this is and I think it's going to be good.' How will I live without her, when she grows up and moves away?

———

The AA meeting at the health farm. I said the truth at the door, which was that I had an alcoholic friend and wanted to know how to be useful, but they looked at me with crooked smiles of scepticism and said, 'Come in.'

'The wife was home by herself, wonderin' where I was. I was down the river drinkin' and doin' wheelies with my brother's apprentices. They were the only blokes who'd drink the way I wanted to drink. I was thirty.'

'I didn't know what love was. I got married for the convenience. To have someone to wash my clothes and cook a meal and be there. I can remember the first time I ever sat on the couch with my wife and held her hand. We already had three kids.'

The way they talked frankly about disgusting things: 'spewin' blood, piddlin' in the bed'.

'Once they go to Al-Anon they start kickin' the props out from under you. Before my wife went, if I was sick in the bed she used to clean it up and wash the sheets. But after she started goin', if I was sick she'd pick up me head and drop me face in it.'

At the end of the meeting they all sprang to their feet and recited the prayer.

———

On French TV at F's parents' place we saw an old man who had invented an alarm clock that didn't bother to go off if it was raining (he produced a large plastic bottle with a spray top and squirted it) and a hammer that dispensed bandaids. Another man had devised a toilet seat that weighed you if you sat on it and raised your feet off the ground.

———

Siena, the trattoria, the rain, the free glass of grappa, the cherry red suede shoes I bought him.

In the guest room of the Tuscan house where I lay reading, a small bat clung to the ceiling. Every time I turned a page its ears stood up.

Very early evening. Fifteen or so people in the grassy courtyard outside the Romanesque church. A mild little wind. People's faces softened by the singing of four young monks (three of them wearing glasses). The long grass full of wildflowers, the valley behind, the thin rows of cypresses, some as thin and pointed as sharpened pencils; poppies in a wandering line that followed a broken fence. Sometimes we would turn a corner and see a whole field of them, tilted, casual, like a red dress thrown out to dry. A German boy passed, looked at us with open face, smiled, we said good evening in our various languages, his girlfriend came behind, a sweet and pretty face. Later a full moon. Fireflies. Our host knows the names of flowers.

I am getting better at playing pétanque and even quite enjoy it. I never can care about winning but I like the effort of getting the boule up to the bouchon. I must be a boring opponent. Glenn Gould says that competition rather than money is the root of all evil.

He said that since his first short story had been accepted by a magazine he didn't need to go on writing: he had proved that he was capable of having his work published.
    'Proved to whom?' said his friend, looking shocked. 'To yourself, or to the world?'
    'It's the same thing, isn't it?'

When I got home the house was dirty and disorderly. I went straight out and bought four nice towels, soap, toothpaste, and a new rubbish bin to replace the green one, which had been stolen *without anyone noticing*. I also called a mechanic and had the leaking washing machine fixed. Today's great achievement: I scrubbed the kitchen walls. They look wonderful, all cream and smooth.

———

He sent me a postcard from Amsterdam: a Daumier drawing from a series called *Moeurs Conjugales*, a man and a woman in two armchairs, their faces distorted by huge, ugly yawns.

———

I showed B my short stories in manuscript. She flipped through it, and remarked on the plastic folder the stories were in, but said nothing about the stories themselves.

———

C and I drove to the Botanic Gardens. I took her arm and we strolled around. I mentioned the Penguin cocktail party and she was mortified that she hadn't been invited. She thought it might cheer her up to see the cactus garden. For the first time, in a real gardener's company, I was able to *look* at these plants, which had always left me cold: their extraordinary obsessive patterns, their shocking excrescences and sudden colours, the subtlety of their black tips and serrated edges.

———

'They asked me,' said P, '"How do you like the picture of yourself in Helen's story?" They were pushing me to outrage.'

I lost my temper. I kicked a tree, a rubbish bin. They think of themselves as artists, as writers. What do they think artists DO? She was laughing; she had seen it before it was published, and had liked it. But I suppose seeing the story in print causes a different kind of pain about oneself from simply reading it in manuscript. Am I a kind of monster? If I am, then Frank Moorhouse and Nadine Gordimer and Raymond Carver are monsters too: 'It's a jungle out there.' I resolve not to defend myself, not even to indulge my rage and fear in coldness.

The Children's Bach is shortlisted for the Victorian Premier's Award. It's a lot of money, fifteen grand or so. I don't know who I'm up against but *I want that prize*.

'Don't get too hopeful, though, Helen,' says M earnestly. 'Just in case.'

K and I ate room service food, sitting on the edge of the single bed like two good children.

M goes to the Melbourne High social, all chic in black.

'You look as pretty as a picture.'

'Thank you, Helen.'

I went and had my hair absolutely CHOPPED.

A tremendous cold northerly blew all day. We drove to St Kilda and walked out on the pier. The air was so clear it was almost frightening: distance had ceased to exist. Closeness of the city buildings, iron grey, all their detail visible.

He'll be like the Russians: he'll retreat and retreat and retreat until I freeze to death.

'After this she was born and re-born with incredible swiftness as a woman, as an imp, as a dog, and finally as a flower. She was some nameless, tiny bell, growing in a stream, with a stalk as fine as hair and a human voice. The water flowing through her flower throat made her sing all day a little monotonous song, "*Kulalla, kulalla,*

kulalla, ripitalla, kulalla, kulalla, kulalla, kulalla, kulla".' —Antonia White, *Beyond the Glass*

Thought I'd finished my *Postcards* manuscript and drove over to McPhee Gribble to deliver it. I hung around their pleasant office for an hour, fiddling with the pages, not wanting to part with them. I became dissatisfied with one of the Paris stories and saw it would not do. Deflated, I went home, where I rummaged through an old folder and found a sheet of paper with one sentence scribbled on it: 'We heard he was back.' Ooh, that Sydney wedding—a story about gossip, about someone who leaves his social group behind. It came pouring out, as short stories sometimes do. I tried to abstract it, to smash it into sharp pieces. I kept thinking of Ania Walwicz's broken sentences, the shock and wit of them.

My problems are never syntactic.

Clear statement: I have very strong urges (irresistible urges) towards some kind of religious or, rather, spiritual experience. This frightens me, not because the spirituality in things is so inscrutable but because I don't know what it will do to my ordinary life arrangements, my friendships, my attitude towards my work, if I turn around and acknowledge something I privately refer to as 'the mighty force'. It's there behind me, and in me, all the time. It's benevolent, it's totally *good*—not morally—I mean that it only wishes me well. But I'm afraid to find out what I'll become if I stop running away from it. It's as if I were always swimming against a tide. How do I turn round and face it? How's it *done*?

My sister talked about reading the Gospels again. The woman at the well was the first person to whom Jesus revealed himself as Messiah.

Women were at the foot of the cross. Women entered the empty tomb. 'It's *all there*,' she said, 'and we've let ourselves be talked out of it.'

But I can't go to church. It would be like going back to Dad, to being an angry daughter.

———

'Solitude is not something you must hope for in the future. Rather, it is a deepening of the present, and unless you look for it in the present you will never find it.' —Thomas Merton

———

This morning, between waking and waking, while sun and wind blew into my room, I dreamt I was going to move to another room in this house. A room I didn't know existed before, although it turned out to be the little white one I had at Capel Street. I was going to have nothing in it but my bed.

———

Finished *Wise Blood*, which I do not understand, and which began somehow to sicken me, all its characters warped and ugly, twisted with ignorance and bad motives and sin.

———

Got proofs of the short stories. Proofs always disappoint me: I hope for beauty, or enlightenment, but it's the same old *matter*.

———

On TV a doco about black gospel singers in Alabama. The old men teaching the young ones the dense harmonies *by ear*, taking them over and over it; the very old men's faces shiny, hard-skinned, reserved, almost noble. A group of women in robes with hoods hanging down their backs—the weirdest singing, with a kind of free, tense rhythm, wild-sounding yet perfectly controlled—the story of the TEW little fishes and the FAHVE loaves of bread.

———

'You're very calm today,' said Q.

'It's false.'

I'm more anxious about what I'll wear to the prize dinner than about whether I'll win or not.

The winner must have known: as soon as his name was read out, a door at the back of the hall burst open and a trolley loaded with copies of his book was trundled in. After the announcement, one of the women judges was nice to me in a way I privately found humiliating. The former ambassador, his devilish good looks somewhat the worse for wear, put his arm across the back of my chair, looked right into my face with an expression of sparkling, malevolent curiosity, and said, showing all his teeth, 'And how are *you* feeling?' It was hard to keep smiling but I hope I managed it. And in my heart I knew that even one of the winning stories knocked my dry, sparse tale into a cocked hat. I know I'm good, but I'm not in his league. Not yet, anyway.

A man tells me he has cards and letters his parents sent to each other. He says he doesn't feel like reading the letters. Perhaps he doesn't want to lose the state of having a secret from himself; or to reach the end of the mystery, the bottom of the bag.

'Oxford Street's Babylon, mate,' says the born-again. 'It's the pit.'

I agree to take part in an ABC radio discussion about 'the future of personal relationships'. 'But why did they invite *you*?' says F. 'What do *you* know about the subject? What made you accept?' He goes to work. I call him and we discuss it further. My voice is shrill and trembly. His is small and vague, as if he were really not all that interested and were even reading something as we spoke.

―――

In the discussion I ran the line against possessiveness that we thought was so cool in the seventies: 'Jealousy is a completely useless emotion.'

Psychoanalyst: 'On the contrary. I think jealousy is at the cutting edge of the psyche.'

Me: (*riveted*) 'What do you mean?'

Psychoanalyst: 'It's painful, but it shows us in no uncertain terms that we are not rational beings. That our lives are not under our conscious control.'

―――

I went outside. I thought wildly of going back to Melbourne, to Geelong, anywhere, hitch-hiking, but it was 10 pm, dark and clouded, and a dog was barking next door. I could hear his heavy boots, he seemed to be walking from one end of the house to the other. I was scared even of walking to the road overlooking the water. I stood with my hands in my pockets and then I came back inside.

―――

He tells me that the vision of life that's in my work is not real; it's much less bad, dark, mischievous, painful etc than real life. It holds out some belief in the essential goodness of people. It is a picture of the way I'd like life to be rather than the way it really is.

'I'm afraid your pessimism will contaminate me,' I say.

'If you believe in good, why are you afraid that bad will contaminate you?'

It's like arguing with the devil.

―――

'She was scarcely still for ten minutes at a time and appeared to have excellent control of her high and hard temper.' —Christina Stead, *Letty Fox, Her Luck*

'That was nice soup we had, wasn't it.'

'Yes but I didn't like the salad.'

'But did you *like* the *soup*.'

'I *said yes*.'

I tried to be ordinary but everything I said sounded false.

'You won't tell me what's wrong. I keep asking, and you won't *tell* me.'

'But that's the problem. You keep *asking* me. You don't ask the right question—you push, push, push, all the time.'

At least I wore my white shoes all day.

The hush of attention, at the literary conference, that comes when someone reads a poem. Everyone is still, even those who have fidgeted during the paper's argument. I love this silence and feel it to be precious.

'I should have gone out,' said the poet casually, 'and found myself a man or two, to make me feel better about myself. But the few I liked were unavailable. So I had to get better by myself. It took longer.'

I said I thought it was probably a more lasting recovery, 'like a very long diet instead of a series of crash ones'.

The barman was a middle-aged Chinese man in horn-rimmed spectacles. We asked for margaritas. He said he didn't know how to make them—did we? One of the academics did, and told him. 'This is inter-esting,' said the barman, keenly following instructions, having a bash at salting the rims. I thought him a remarkable person.

F brings home a video of a wonderful concert in Managua. We sit in a row to watch it. He leans forward eagerly. A handsome woman with a black chignon and blazing white teeth all the way down her throat sings in a wild, flamboyant voice a song about revolution. If we'd been alone I would have said to him, 'According to your picture of the world and of art, the only song worth her singing would say "Fight as you may, peasant comrades, you will be crushed like beetles between the super-powers. Your land will be defoliated and your children slaughtered."'

Why do I persist? I have no hope left. I conclude that I persist out of fear.

A stranger actually writes me a letter urging me not to become a Christian. I throw it in the bin.

In the kitchen at the publisher's party the novelist talked about a movie he wants to write. I sat and listened to him talk himself into being too scared to do it and then out again.

The African-American feminist's announcement that she would read last was brought to us by one of the organisers as we milled about before the session began. We all deferred without a murmur, though I had read enough of her work to know it was ploddingly didactic. She assumed that we were ignorant of terms such as 'mortar', 'pestle', 'gay', 'Lucky Strike': before enlightening us she would make a little fence over her mouth with one hand and murmur, 'Culture break'. But when she spoke to me, down in the seats, she seemed an ordinary human being, likeable and warm.

Trucks rush past outside the motel on the Western Highway. An orange sunset impressed my father. He leaned his elbows on the metal rail and stared at it, then returned to his room to tear another handful of flesh off the cold chicken he had brought with us from Highton. He flips the bones over the railing into the carpark. Next day, as we drive on, he says, "Member those chicken bones I chucked over the rail? This morning they were all gone. Must be cats. Or rats.'

―――――

I turned on the TV and saw a woman having her baby delivered by caesarean. I burst into tears when they lifted the tiny thing out: a girl, her head covered in that grey waxy stuff, her legs bent and weak. They weighed her, cleared out her breathing passages—a close-up of the little head in profile, eyes stuck down tight, mouth gaping, the plastic tube being pushed down her throat by two huge hands in surgical gloves. They put a white cotton cap on her head and wrapped her in silver paper, exactly like a fish fillet for the oven.

―――――

My father describes a woman we know as 'a very attractive girl, a very *precise* girl, with a polished voice'. Delighted with these adjectives, I look away. Next he uses the expression 'not privy to'. Maybe, if I lie low and listen, he'll let out a grand vocabulary that he's been hiding all his life.

―――――

When he addresses a stranger he uses no preliminary attention-getting phrase like 'Excuse me'. He just walks up behind them and starts talking. 'Where would the supermarket be?' 'Take long to walk into town from here, does it?' 'Got any orange squeezers?' His voice seems very loud and deep in public places.

'This is the worst town I've been in for—'
'*Shhh*! Lower your voice!'

I'm surprised to find he has strong views on the treatment of Aboriginal people. 'See? *Aboriginal Reserve*,' he says, with his big flat fingertip on the map. 'Right up north. Where it doesn't rain.'

On the Ghan, an endless night of trundling, rattling, bumping, shivering of fittings, and occasionally, between fitful periods of sleep, sightings of tremendous, dense panoplies of stars. At dawn horizontal stripes of morning sun run brokenly along the bushes. In the night I finished *Seven Poor Men of Sydney*. I'm shocked. I never knew Stead was a visionary. (What does that word mean?) Beside her I am a dwarf, scared, narrow, a timid shallow burrower.

The timidity, the ugly clothing of the travellers on the train. Cheap, gristle-soled shoes, home-made cardigans in a variety of browns and oranges and beiges. To see a decent pair of old brogues or proper leather shoes is a reprieve from murderous contempt. I'm poised to despise; my smiles are false. A man walked through the bar carrying a copy of the *Age Monthly Review*. I longed to run after him and his wife and kid.

On the platform at Port Augusta, a big group of black women with their children. Their stick-like legs, some marked with ulcers and scabs, their big runners and tennis socks pulled up, their loose synthetic dresses and football beanies, their large stomachs, their big breasts that hang down over their bellies, their straw-like curly hair. The babies' top lips gleam with silver snot. They were going to sit up all night in economy.

My father is incapable of conversation. His speech is almost rhetorical: he speaks very slowly, with the emphases of someone giving important information to a listener whose understanding he has no faith in. Any topic that comes up is quickly put aside as soon as his opinion has been delivered. If I try to keep it going he makes no response. I wonder if my tone becomes hectoring. We batted ideas (dull lumps, but all we had to play with) across the table for an hour or so. I felt by comparison quite light on my feet, whereas usually in argument I am blurred, slow, opinionless. I brought my case around in a big circle and closed it; I felt the satisfaction of form. I felt also unscrupulous, even ashamed.

———

He doesn't like my driving. When I stalled on a stony rise near the ochre pits, he clicked his tongue and took the wheel. The gorge: beautiful white gums, slate-green water riffled by a strong dry northerly. No one in sight. Sandals, two big pairs and two small, in a neat row on the bank, like the remains of a family suicide.

———

He says his father was one of thirteen children. Various tales of wills capriciously changed, or changed under malicious influence. The cousin whose father wouldn't let her marry the man she loved, and who would have been a Lady by now. The aunt who's weak and whose children and grandchildren sponge off her. Fascinating but drily told, not in the juicy way one longs for—no sense of the real lives of people, just wooden figures being moved about on a board.

———

Why am I here? I thought it was to find my father, but maybe it's to connect with a power so much bigger than he is that it will free me from him.

———

I dreamt about a new house. In the room that was to be mine I found a dead body lying on its back in a long cardboard carton under the table. I pulled it out by its ankles. Its leg bones were split open lengthwise and in their furrows lay, end to end, dozens of brand-new biros, Bic medium-point, the transparent plastic sort. They rattled around and tipped out when the body was moved.

I told Dad the dream. At the bit about the biros we laughed, and he said, 'How many did you take?'

———

I climbed the rock at dawn with a London barrister who arrived at the base on a motorbike just as I got out of the car. One of those floppy-haired Englishmen with pink cheeks and fine features. Hurray! The first person I'd met in a week with whom small talk was not necessary. It was a hard climb and I started along the chain too fast. I tasted blood. 'We'll take plenty of rests,' said the barrister. The wind was powerful and very cold and I didn't have enough clothes on, but my heavy boots were suited to the job. The two Japanese kids coming down, gasping with wonder: 'We—saw—many stars! We—saw—*comets*!'

———

You can't write about this stuff. I met my Mighty Force on top of the rock and it played with me.

———

'She's got a season ticket,' said Dad. 'She likes to go to concerts. She likes classical music. Oh, I like it too, but—I reckon you can have too much of that sort of thing.' The idea of excess; how he hates it. I walked out to see the sun go down, and passed the bar, from which poured loud music and voices, like the noise of a party. I glanced in, saw dimness, many men in working clothes, some bending over pool tables. I loved the noise. I thought gladly that somewhere people were shouting, talking to each other, *over-doing it*. I looked round and saw a clapped-out Valiant with two mattresses and some bendy strips of building materials strapped to the roof. In the front seat sat three men in singlets, dust-coated, sunburnt. I smiled and waved, and so did they. The driver planted his foot and the car took off in a plume of dust. The motor sounded sick, the man was laughing, I laughed too and off I went, running and jumping and swinging my arms. 'Ratbags!' I shouted to myself, a tribute to maniacs and excess.

———

Corny, mediocre country-and-western songs that touch on painful truth.

———

My father lives on meat.

———

At the base of the rock the silence plugs my ears. There are no sounds. Then a little tuft of grass behind me rustles. I jump round. Other clumps hiss and move, it is a sudden rush of wind, my skin stands up.

———

Oh, how we hang on to that last prison! Even though it's ugly and damaging.

———

I felt stranger and stranger. I took a cab to North Sydney. In the hotel a strange wind whined at the window and what water I could see was mistral-coloured. I sat looking out at the warm evening, the sparkling towers, and thought in a stunned way, This is a very peculiar moment in my life.

———

I could say to him, 'I would get a broken heart if you left. But it's been broken before, and has healed.'

———

In the funding meetings they probably think I am 'tough and ruthless', but they are mistaking for ruthlessness a spontaneous following of my shit-detector, which is the only part of me that functions confidently in this impersonal world.

A poem translated from the Arabic called *Homesickness*. Words to the effect of 'Once again you take out your knife and stab me', and then this: *'Nobody knows whether I am dancing or staggering.'*

'There is something between me and her.'
   'Since when?'
   'Two weeks.'
I keep walking but put my hands in my pockets.
Nobody knows whether I am staggering or dancing.

It is night. Perhaps it is raining, or has been. He stands with my suitcase in his hand, and looks wildly for his car. The car park is half empty, but he cannot see it. 'I think it has been stolen,' he says. 'Look again,' I say. 'It must be here.' And it is, white and long, slightly closer to the building than he has remembered.

He has been tormented for a long time by childlessness.

I'm split in two: the shocked, stunned part which will suffer when feeling returns, and another part which examines and censors certain urges that rise thickly and clumsily from the stunned part: no, that is a cheap shot; no, there you are drawing attention to yourself as suffering; no, it would not be just to say that, and so on.

I slept about two hours, woke at 5.30 in my room and watched the curtains get whiter.

'You never made concessions to me, in the way you lived your life.' This I cannot deny.

Downstairs M and the two girls from Ballarat have set up their music stands and are playing eighteenth-century music with sweetness and confidence. I love their straight backs, their gay clothes, their lovely concentration. 'Again? Two, three, *four*.'

———

I was hard inside, bitter and cold, wanting to hurt her: 'If you'd been fifty-three, ugly and stupid, this wouldn't have happened.' But she went on being humble. She turned the other cheek, is that it? She went on standing there, presenting herself, not running away.

———

'People who are jealous,' he said, 'ask questions whose answers will hurt them. That's why I lied.'

———

'I'm sorry,' I said. 'I've hurt you terribly.'
  'But I have hurt *you* much worse than that.'
  'Let's forgive each other.'
  'I forgive you for everything.'
  'I forgive you too, for everything.'
  All this through sobs, and floods of tears. And then we went out into the kitchen and started drinking.

———

The girls played, and I washed the dishes, wearing the grotesque rubber gloves my sister brought me from New York, with the silver ring and painted nails. I finished the scotch. I went to bed. I read a poem by Alison Clark called *Credo*: 'I *am* chained, but I have a soul…' And then I went to sleep.

———

M's father, F and me walking in the cemetery with the dog.
  Now I have two ex-husbands.

———

Strange images of loneliness: a bathroom that's *clean*, with a hollow sound because it contains only two towels, hers and mine.

In the old woman's calm flat, full of her quiet, idiosyncratic, practical objects and things of unusual colour, she too was calm. Women who live alone and like it have a rested, full look. I told her everything. 'It seems,' she said, 'that when you are successful you need to have someone near who will undercut you. As if you will not allow yourself to flower fully.'

In the wine bar F put to me his proposition. I stayed firm, but felt inside the small screaming sadness of having to reject something you long for but which is offered in a wrong spirit.

I need to find out why I so often get myself into situations where people have to symbolically murder me.

My little niece's collection of matchboxes, full of obsessively modelled plasticine objects. Each box has a label: 'CONTAINS: Carrot. Guitar'. I want to burst out laughing with each treasure she unveils, her intricate inspirations. I long to make a little movie, to show her absorbed expression, the way her head comes forward on her neck to peep into the next container.

'My experience tells me that marriage does not make one happier. It takes away the illusion that had sustained a deep belief in the possibility of a kindred soul.' —Paula Modersohn-Becker in her diary, 1902

'...Layers, or strata, or veils; an indefinable looseness or flexibility of handling; windows; autobiographical content; animals, flowers; a certain kind of fragmentation; a new fondness for the pinks and pastels and ephemeral cloud colours that used to be tabu unless a woman wanted to be accused of making "feminine" art…' —Lucy Lippard on recurring elements in women's art, in *From the Center*

Leave me alone. I'll get over you if you'll just leave me alone.

A drunken, filthy old man walked straight off the street into R's house. He thought it was *his* place. We pushed him gently out the front door. He sat on the pavement shouting: 'I kill. I kill everything.' After half an hour he got up and walked away.

A voice almost oily with the desire to appear co-operative.

'When my husband and I split up,' the woman told me, 'he suddenly wanted to talk at great length about himself. He used to invite me over and cook a meal and have a bottle of wine, and start pouring out streams of stuff. I used to feel so terribly tired, and bored, that I'd fall asleep at the table.'

'Because it was too late?'

'Yes—and because instead of tinkering all along, the way women do with their friends, he wanted to produce one great dollop, and expected me to pick it up and carry it. And I couldn't, and didn't want to.'

Traces of his presence: large, hacked scraps of toenail on the bedcovers. I picked them up with care. Lucky for him I'm not a witch.

Fresh morning. I went for a jog in Princes Park. Elms still fluttering and shedding those very pale green seedpods: they make a tiny rustle on the ground when a breeze moves them. Near the football ground a black man, a Pacific Islander I think, was doing stretch exercises after a run. His body was thick, dark, packed solid, shining, in green shorts and a tracksuit top. I *think* that's what he was wearing. How on earth do people give evidence in murder trials?

A houseful of sleeping teenage girls. Bleached hair sticking out of twisted doonas.

I told Z that we'd split up. His reaction was what I'd expected—a rapid drawing-back, a look that said, 'I don't want you to tell me about it, I don't want to know the emotional stuff.'

At Tarrawarra the brown river ran by. In an outside corner of the abbey there was an arsenal of anti-magpie sticks, leaning against the white weatherboards. Each of us carried one in rifle position on the shoulder. Every now and then we would pause and stand still. Always traffic noise, but also the twittering of swallows. The soft, heavy air that hangs over rich farmland. Wheel marks in the grass—on each blade a glossy sheen of light.

The interviewer asked me a strange question: 'In what ways are you a different person from the one you were ten or twenty years ago?'

I could have bawled, but I thought for a long time and then said, in a low voice, 'I know now that people will do anything. They will do *anything*.'

At the Harbourfront International Literary Festival in Toronto I am mistaken by three separate male writers for a staff helper. 'How many buses do you *have*, in this organisation?' 'I've no idea. I don't work for it.' Stanley Elkin, an American writer of 'extravagant, satirical fiction', is offended when I say I have to go straight home after the festival. 'Nobody *has* to do anything.' 'Yes, they do.' 'Why can't you stay a couple of weeks and go to New York?' 'I'd have liked to. But I have to go straight home.' 'But why?' 'Because I split up with my husband just before I came away, and I've got a daughter at home.' That shut him up. But when he found out that my daughter was sixteen he renewed his attack. He moves about on two sticks and has the bitter look of someone in pain.

———

In the gallery I liked humble paintings of interiors. A bedroom, a strip of light across a chest of drawers. It becomes clear to me that middling art comforts, while very good art challenges and unsettles. The Henry Moores, though, do something else: they make you *still*. Your breathing slows down.

———

Two gay shop assistants saying goodbye. The black one says, 'Touch you later.'

———

At Niagara Falls, Kenzaburō Ōe told me a little story. 'A Japanese man came up to me, back there. He said, "Are you Japanese?" I said, "Yes." He showed me his camera and said, "Japanese camera." Then he said, pointing at the falls, "Are you surprised?" I said, "Yes." He turned to his wife and said, "This man is Japanese, and he is surprised."' We laughed so much, we could not stop.

———

The timelessness of a long flight. I gazed down on the land we were passing over. An immensity of absolute flatness, divided by humans into a regular pattern of squares, and planted and cropped. It spread away in every direction for thousands of miles. I was frightened. Every now and then a small town would cluster at an intersection of roads, or in the bend of a river. I thought, Each of these settlements has a name, a social fabric, a *feel* to it all its own which its inhabitants consider to be unique. This thought made my heart ache. We passed over snow-sprinkled mountains, then a wide valley, then a grey, bare wilderness through which twisted seaweed-shaped rivers or dry watercourses.

At 3 am I woke, and came to very gradually. My eyes focused on the top shelf of a bookcase. I thought, 'That looks just like my bookcase at home.' I let my glance roll sideways and down. I saw a planet lamp, a mirror, all these minor, still objects in the faint light from outside the curtains. I was astonished. 'This room, in Canada, is exactly like my room in Melbourne.' Then I woke properly. I was at home, in my own bed. A moment of absolute happiness.

The Exhibition Gardens are thick with new leaves and lovers lying in sexual postures.

The woman at the wedding who told me about the months, even years, after her husband was killed in a car accident. 'Nothing that should have been good was. I'd look out the window in the morning and see the sun shining, but it wasn't good.' Is that what grief is?

On the phone K told me some true-life stories about swords and rings. They were wonderful. I said, 'Why aren't you writing all this down? Without trying to be funny?'

Imagine living in a city beside an OCEAN.

At the pub reading, the lights shone in my eyes and I saw nothing but one young woman's face, right at the back. She was smiling, rapt. It unnerved me. I felt I could not read well enough, had not written well enough, to justify her undefended openness.

―――

I saw the mad one. His face is triangular, like that of a knight in a painting. His eyes slide away.

―――

I wonder if what we see as a world full of couples is really a world of triangles.

―――

The dream where someone gave me three Swiss knives, big, middle-sized, small.

―――

I get no pleasure out of drinking. I feel blurred, stunned, disconnected, after even the tiniest quantity. I've got pains. Shoulders stiff as coathangers. My neck is rigid. My ovaries hurt. My tubes hurt. The twinges are tube-shaped.

―――

The meeting at the Goethe-Institut. Openable windows, huge pale green leaves thickly massed outside the glass. The motherly woman stood next to me with her hand on my shoulder. Her kindness made my self-control almost impossible to maintain. I longed to burst out sobbing, to lean my face against the arm of the tall man beside me, and for people to go on talking quietly and let me be weak. But *the show had to go on*. She pointed to my head and said, 'You've got a real little puritan in there, haven't you!'

―――

I dreamt I saw a white bird, like a pigeon, waddling along a path with a smaller white bird riding on its head, and the second white bird had an even smaller bird perched on *its* head, a bird that was of a striated appearance, black and white, like a stone or a streaky opal. People watched and laughed indulgently, as at a clever circus trick or a childish antic.

―――

It is always me who ends our phone calls. Sometimes I feel boredom creeping over me, but K could chatter on till nightfall.

———

I feel: disgusted. Angry, jealous, tired. Bored. But all in quantities so small as to make action or even statement too much of an effort.

———

Dreamt I was in India, in a room full of children. The window was open. A jeep full of soldiers drove past. One of them stood up and threw a hand grenade into the room. I turned away and covered my head. One of the older boys picked up the grenade and threw it back out. A close-up of the grenade as it lay on the floor: it looked black and greasy, and its surface was divided into those raised squares one sees in cartoon drawings of such manly objects.

———

M got 97% for French. She's going to Paris next week. In the park she left her coat on a rail and did cartwheels and somersaults on the grass.

———

'Perhaps it is better that men don't grow up,' said the Polish doctor. 'When they do they become sad, and serious.' Is this why women are sad? Because they are obliged to grow up? They have children, they shoulder the emotional responsibility and let the men go free?

———

A letter comes. Another description, from someone I love, of me as too big to handle.

———

I dreamt I went to the doctor complaining of a nasty discharge. She approached me with a pair of scissors. 'You're not going to cut my hair, are you?' I cried. She insisted, good-humouredly, and I let her. I shut my eyes while she clipped. When I opened them and looked in the mirror I was surprised to find I looked all right. Fragile, almost pretty, like someone recovering from a dangerous illness.

———

The old writer read a story full of flip stuff, lists of expensive things—cars, furniture, whisky—and tales of faithless wives. I watched two women in the front row. As he read, their faces registered a polite distaste.

———

The way P had put watercolour on the paper made tears of respect come to my eyes. A picture of a centaur in a ring of moonlit trees had the same effect on me as a book I remember reading as a child, illustrated by Edward Ardizzone: some children in a moonlit garden, silvery and mysterious and terrifying.

———

I have stopped cracking hardy. I cry, I shout. Last night I reached the lowest moment. I went into the kitchen, I didn't turn on the light. I stood at the sink and ran myself a glass of water, but I was crying so hard my mouth was too stiff to drink. I was full of shame and cheapness and misery.

———

The painter told me that when she finished the portrait she 'sat down in the lumpy chair and cried'. The miracle of making something that wasn't there before. Pulling something out of thin air.

———

I cried a bit more and then I ate my breakfast and read the paper. A stubborn optimism came creeping into me as I climbed the stairs. I went and had a healthy shit. I got out my new Hermes and set it up with pleasure.

———

I pulled the petals off the pink roses, which were almost dead. I seized each bloom with my fingertips and pulled: they came away with a little fleshy helpless resistance.

I dreamt of a church. A spiritual possibility in living alone, with children but without a man. I ate about a kilo of cherries, all by myself, without having to feel guilty for *not sharing*.

—

I wanted to say, 'Can I come over?' But I was too proud.

—

I am by myself. I think I like it but I'm not sure. It's 'good for me'.

—

It is always worse to see your mother lie down and take it than to see her stand up and start yelling.

—

The old woman showed us a photo of herself on holiday in America, standing on a country road in summer wearing a dress that reached halfway down her calves—an abundant skirt, a loose blouse and flat sandals. Her legs were comfortably spaced, her feet planted firmly. 'It's *you!* You look wonderful. You look like a peasant woman.' She simpered, back home in her Melbourne eastern suburbs outfit of a neat-cut synthetic frock, sheer stockings, and prissy little high-heeled sandals that made her stance like that of a bird gripping a twig.

—

Went to Communion. The Mighty Force is not there. Or it doesn't stand near me. The bread and wine don't seem to have anything to do with it. Or maybe it's me, awkward on my knees, anxious about doing or saying the wrong thing among those pretty, slender, grey-haired ladies who genuflect.

—

Twenty years ago, at uni, but I knew her at once. The long Italian boots, the brown wool dress. The face: closed, dark, in pain. The hands in pockets, the fast, absorbed walk, head down.

—

We say hurtful things that are not quite true. Such a war. Ammunition to hand in any situation. Any memory can be distorted at will.

———

He drove away. I stood at the gate. His face remained turned towards me until he was swallowed up in the dark.

———

They told me that no English publisher is interested in my work. A bloke with a hyphenated name said, having read *The Children's Bach* and *Postcards from Surfers*, that he 'just didn't like the stuff'. Why does this make me cry? Why should I *care*?

———

The doctor's kindness and intelligence make his face attractive. He said that the medical politics surrounding AIDS was 'disgusting'. He said that at the hospital they got attached to the AIDS patients. 'It's awful. They *all die*. Every one of them. Young men, never had a day's sickness in their lives. It's sad. It's as if your brothers and sisters kept on dying.' He said the gay men in the AIDS task force 'had a hidden agenda: basically, underneath, they claim it as a right that they should be able to fuck any man they choose. That's all right, except when you've got a fatal disease.'

———

I read in the *New Yorker* that Rosario Godoy, a member of an organisation of women searching for 'disappeared ones' in Guatemala, was found dead in a car that had crashed over a cliff. Also in the car were her brother and her infant son, both dead. It might have been passed off as an accident but for one thing: the baby's fingernails had been pulled out.

———

K calls and wants to change all the arrangements.
    'We've had our deadlines brought forward. They sprang it on us at the weekend.'

'Why didn't you ring up at the weekend and tell me?'

'I had all my *shopping* to do,' he says irritably, 'and then I was at a *party*.'

A strange little orgasm, a keeping-still orgasm, brought about by a sudden mind-sight of a museum, an art gallery, a wall filled to the sides with a rapid series of intense and highly-coloured paintings. All this, however, as if experienced by someone else, which explains my reluctance to use 'I' in an account of it. Now that K's gone, and I'm in the hotel room by myself, I can't find any trace of his having been here: as if the hours of his visit existed in some element other than the time which is now in force.

A rainstorm, with hail and thunder, passed over. It blotted out the harbour entirely. It was strange to see the raindrops from this far (eleven storeys) above the ground: they fell past the window in an apparent order, each in its own column of air, not jostling or swerving. I fell asleep watching a tap-dancing movie on TV.

I'm scared.

I'd like to be able to accept my physical self as it is. I resist being looked at. I want to be the controlling one, the one who looks.

The harbour pool, Balmain, with two women, a producer and a director, who want to make a movie with me. Grey water slapping, a salty smell like Eastern Beach in Geelong. We swam about, calling to each other and laughing. From the dressing sheds, if we stood on the seats, we could look out through louvres and see the low port buildings all peaceful in the grey rainy evening. We walked up the steep hill under the trees. A strong smell of moss.

I remembered my body, that I was alive in the physical world.

———

'Gosh, you're prolific, aren't you!'

'Lately I am—but I'm always lashing myself for being lazy.'

———

I told the Jungian about Dad, his mother dying when he was two. 'A child who loses his mother,' he said, 'is often unable to trust anyone, ever again.'

———

Wonderful landscapes, full of grain—shades of blond—and tremendous clouds, richly shaped, with dark floors and boiling white tops. Sometimes a split, through which a clear blue would show or, further west, a paler pastel greenish-blue.

———

She saves used teabags. She uses every teabag twice. I refuse to believe she's that poor.

———

A horrible dream about sex with a man whose face as we fucked turned beast-like: the eyes sank into the skull, moved closer together, burned with a red light. I knew that this creature wanted to murder me, and that I had some secret power which could hold its savagery under control as long as I went on *believing* I had this power.

———

The student told me about speed, cocaine.

'Do you mean snorting?'

'No. Hitting. My boyfriend was dealing, he had enough money for us to *go right down*. I went right to the bottom, really quickly. And came up again. I feel I've got that stuff out of the way.'

'Do your parents know?'

'I told Mum. She said, "Should I be worried?" and I said, "No, you shouldn't."'

I was getting dressed after my swim when I heard the woman on the turnstile say, 'He's got all his clothes on!' Running steps, the PA hissed, and a scornful, angry male voice, highly amplified, said, 'Will that man in his clothes *get out of the water.* GET OUT NOW.' I came out to look. A sodden man with thick dark hair, in jeans and a shirt and shoes, was sitting in the posture of Rodin's Thinker on a starting block, with his back to the water, passing one spread hand back and forth across his forehead. 'He's a flip,' said the woman at the turnstile. 'He's a flip. He's got something wrong with him.'

Could I write a story without any characters? Only objects?

I bought some red leather sandals and some pink ballet shoes.

'Cod seemed a suitable dish for a rejected one and I ate it humbly without any kind of sauce or relish.' —Barbara Pym, *Excellent Women*. This is Elizabeth Jolley's tone and it made me laugh out loud.

At Parsley Bay I hit my right knee very hard against an underwater concrete step. It hurt so much that things went colourless.

T and I agreed that we liked having short hair, and didn't feel very female. She told me she had read a Jungian book about goddesses, and bought herself some skirts. 'But in a while I got sick of them. They don't have pockets. And what are you supposed to wear on your feet and legs?' I lent her the Kombi. She stole some bricks in it, went home and built a barbecue, then rang and asked me to dinner. She cooked two trout on the coals.

Q's patient demeanour makes me ashamed of the pleasure I take in complaining, in being aggrieved.

———

The murdered girl's stepfather told us that at the committal hearing the two accused were sitting right in front of him. 'They were holding hands and giggling. All my principles about capital punishment went out the window. Immediately. *Straight away.*'

Another friend at the table said, 'Do you want to get inside their heads?'

A long pause.

'No. I've never wanted that. Because it might make me feel—'

'Merciful?'

'No! Not merciful. I'm afraid it would be like going through the gates of hell. I'm afraid that if I found what violence and cold-bloodedness there was in *their* heads, I might find the same thing in myself.'

The other man tried to argue with him about this—to comfort him, to reassure him that he could never be as bad as that. But he would not be persuaded. Secretly I admired him for it.

'Everybody in my position,' he said, 'wants to be asked the questions we can't ask ourselves.' He said they want to be *pushed*, but they are concerned not to tell people things they might not be able to handle. 'You're scared you'll make them feel worse than you do yourself.'

I asked him if I could come to the trial.

'Why do you want to?'

'First because I thought you might like people to be with you. And second because I'm curious.'

The real truth would be in reverse order. In fact the real truth is part 2. The first is cosmetic, though it *is* true also, in another way.

Each of us sat with her chair turned slightly towards the open back door. The baby is due in five weeks. Upstairs I saw the baby's things. I loved the singlets best of all: white cotton, size 000, with a rib. Something in Elizabeth Jolley about the pangs caused by the sight of a baby's shoulders. I remember the shoulders, and the pangs.

Someone's applied to rent our spare room, a law student, and M's school friend's big brother.

'Is he a spunk?'

'Not when you first see him. But then you realise he is.'

'What's their family like?'

'A bit like us. They eat crude things. Nobody's much of a cook. Once I asked her if she wanted some pastrami and matzos, and she looked blank. I showed her what it was and she said, "At our place we call that meat and bread."'

C calls me from a restaurant in St Kilda. 'My father's just told me: a nudnik is a bore. A shlemiel is an idiot. And a shmendrick is a born loser.'

I told the Jungian how I hated and feared the kind of privilege claimed by beautiful women.

'And how have *you* claimed attention, Helen?'

I did not like being asked this question.

'Sex. Using my brains.'

Swimming laps at 8 pm. The cold, when I get out of the water, makes my jaw go up and down like that of a ventriloquist's dummy.

Tenant number 2. A, a born-again, from Sydney. Heavy eyelids, hair that grows in points in front of his ears, a slow naughty wit and an old-world turn of phrase: 'Don't give 'em too much leeway or they'll skin you.' The girls ask what makes black bread black. 'It's probably got molasses in it,' he says. I inspect the packet. 'There's no mention of molasses on this list of ingredients.' He snatches it from my hand with a snarl: 'Gimme a look at that label.' I seize the uke and defiantly play *There Is a Fountain Filled with Blood*. Maybe this could become a household.

———

I reviewed Spalding Gray's one-man show. Last night he came up to me in the lobby and shook my hand, asked for my phone number. Up close his eyes looked unnaturally wide apart, as if they didn't focus or as if he'd had something to drink, or smoke. The audience loved him and I felt proprietary.

———

Space Shuttle Challenger blew up just after blast-off. The 'first school-teacher in space' was thus vaporised before the eyes of her pupils, parents, husband and children. The strange shape of the exploded stuff—white smoke etc. It was pretty horrible but I felt revolted after a while by the emotional tirades the US media carried on with.

———

The woman's husband, whom she deeply loved, has died. She wrote: 'I feel I have been reborn without skin on an alien planet.'

———

The teenager told us that when she heard that her parents were going to separate, she pulled the new wallpaper off her bedroom walls. 'I tore it all down with my fingernails. I didn't even know I was doing it. I suddenly saw—' She mimes waking up and looking at her outstretched hands as if they held strips of paper.

———

The mind of A, the born-again, has several gears: dreamy and disconnected; witty and on the ball; plodding with difficulty from point to point in some long internal argument of which only the iceberg tips emerge in speech: 'There's worse things than war.'

―――

The gist of it is, I guess, that I wasn't vulnerable, or feminine. F says that I didn't need him enough, that I barged straight through him. I have to accept this in silence. Because it is true.

―――

I am a forty-three-year-old woman, a mother, healthy, reasonable-looking; I am in my own city; I am able to make a living; I am sometimes sad or frightened, and recently I have been hurt; but I am also learning to examine myself and my crimes less defensively; the Mighty Force has not lately come to me in the form I was expecting; but it does not abandon people, and it won't abandon *me*.

―――

Spalding Gray, the monologist. He talks *all the time*. But since he is never boring, one is never bored. His voice is 'soft, pleasant and emphatic'. He has a strange face, rather like a dog's: big-mouthed and snubbed. He says he is very drawn to the neuroses of women: 'I'm always acting out stuff with my mother, who killed herself in 1967.' A woman approached him in Sydney. 'It was getting too much for me so I left the bar without saying anything. Next morning she left a note in my box: "That was a pretty tacky thing to do." She even came to my hotel when I wasn't there and asked the clerk for my *key*.' He gave me a copy of his book and wrote in it, having to ask me to check his spelling: 'Thank you for shinning your lights on me.' I suppose he meant what I wrote about him in the newspaper. We talked for several hours. I've never met a more fully and richly self-obsessed person in all my life.

―――

I listened and listened. Did I hear? Maybe not what the man was telling me, or wanting to impart; but something.

―――

The law student washed the dishes last night, without speed, enthusiasm or skill.

―――

A day at the murder trial, in the Supreme Court. At first bored with the nit-picking and the slow pace, but after a while we became accustomed to the rhythm and entered into the case's *world*. The feast of human types dragged in as witnesses: two junkies; a man from Glen Waverley; a union official and his wife, a toughie with a cigaretty voice, long perfect silver nails which she tapped loudly on the witness stand, a carefully tended tan, long arms and legs, slender, very well-preserved (younger than me, no doubt). After this I was terribly tired, almost ecstatic with fatigue. And I was only *watching*.

―――

They have found at Ayers Rock the body—partly eaten by 'dingoes, birds or goannas'—of a young English tourist who had fallen; and beside or near it *a baby's matinee jacket.*

1986

A told me about his father and his brother. 'I felt that if they couldn't get themselves together they should *die*.' He said it harshly, with a sharp pushing-aside gesture of one hand. Then, of course, they did, and the girl killed herself. 'I just went to bed. I was completely undone. And I prayed. I didn't believe, but I prayed.'

'What did you say?'

'I said, "If there's anybody who can take away this load of guilt, please will you."'

———

'You seem happy lately, sweetheart. Singing round the house, always in a good mood.'

'Yes, I am. It's so much nicer around here. You used to fight *all the time.*'

———

In the cathedral, fifteen minutes before the communion service was to start, a bloke got up and said, 'As we feared, someone has rung a TV station and said there's a bomb in the building.' A boy of five or so was sitting beside me with his mother. At the word 'bomb' he looked up at me with an expression of intense and comical puzzlement, and said, as if trying to nut out a problem, 'Well, it can't be the Americans, because—'

'It's not a bomb from a plane,' I said. 'It's only a stupid joke—somebody's told the police that there's a bomb under a seat.'

He sprang up like a scalded cat, would not be reassured that it was a hoax, and dragged his mother off down the aisle at a fast clip.

———

Another day in court. Fascination seized me. An unflappable pathologist read out her description of the injuries and wounds on the girl's body. The shock of detail.

———

They rang and told me I'd won the festival award. Ten grand. I began to tremble at the knees.

———

I woke and heard the north-westerly rushing the dead leaves past our house: thousands and thousands, an unending supply, a people going into exile. Now the sky over the low mountains is dusty orange.

———

While we were in the Twins it began to thunder and lighten and pour with rain. The dog, chained to the post outside the shop, barked and whined. She did not have the nous to stand under the veranda.

———

P called in at dinner time and ate with us. She spoke about Halley's Comet and suddenly the wonder of its colossal journey struck me. Surely God exists? Can such a phenomenon have no meaning?

———

Dreamt I went to church and sat in a pew. I felt calm, and waited for enlightenment which I knew would come: I didn't have to *do* anything in order to be enlightened, just sit quietly and be ready. A feeling of quietly simmering expectation. Something good and right coming, if I could be patient.

———

The woman accused of the murder must have learned her evidence by heart. Would a girl who says 'somethink' and 'anythink' also say, 'And I think on the odd occasion another female' or 'prior to reaching the service station' or 'the matter that I'd been taken into custody for'? She said she was 're-luke-tant' to do something and her barrister had to correct her. The frightful pathos of this. I would say they were done like a dinner.

The man was found guilty. And the judge directed the jury to acquit the woman because the charge against her could not be proved. We all stood up, incredulous. But then came to me a sharp flash of illumination: what we were bowing to was not this thin, tough-faced man in a red robe, but to the power that he exercised, that passed through him, that our society gives him. I felt the spirit of the law—something tremendous restraining itself by reason. *They really do have to prove it.*

The class reunion, in a suburban backyard. People had brought their husbands. Nobody told me we could, and just as well, for I no longer have one. The men must have been very bored. They barbecued a creature on a spit and stood about drinking. A woman whose quiet, intelligent manner and thick fair hair I vividly remembered told me she was a hypnotherapist: 'I like depressives. Suicides. People in extreme fear states. Schizophrenics.' The woman who was head prefect the year before me, a powerful hockey player, seized my arm: 'I read your book. Saw it on TV. Bloody awful. Sorry. Hated it. Not trying to be rude, but it was bloody awful. You won't get any false praise from *me*.' I shrugged, and folded my arms. She immediately folded hers. It was cold in the garden. Someone passed round an exercise book and we wrote our names. When I saw the way one woman wrote—left-handed, a thin brown claw—I felt a small rush of emotion: 'Oh—the way you hold a pen—I remember it!' People burst into shrieks and cries. I suppose we spent all our school lives together with pens in our hands.

———

Marcos flees the Philippines. Photos of him, mouth agape, orating into a microphone on the palace balcony, and behind him, plump and coiffed and upholstered, the repellent Imelda, her face casting a slanted glance past him as if towards a mob.

———

Pulling on his steel-toed boots, A sings to himself softly, tunefully and correctly, 'Blame It on the Boogie'.

———

The husband talks as if the wife were not present. He considers himself the main act and will cut across her quite ruthlessly, not even noticing he's doing it, in the middle of her sentence. She neither objects nor submits, but lowers her voice slightly and goes on speaking as a subtext to *his* discourse, even though each of them might be talking about something quite different.

———

J's put on a lot of weight and looks brown, smooth and solid. I was so happy to see him, I wanted to curl up under his arm and stay there all day. We lay on the grass listening to the speakers. When I got up I had green duck shit on my linen jacket, and I did not care.

———

They gave me the prize. I had to make a speech. My new black shoes were giving me terrible blisters. Thea Astley gave me some bandaids. She hugged me and said, 'You can write about all those tiny household things, like scraping the food off the cupboard fronts, and *validate* them.' Quite a few people told me that *The Children's Bach* is 'so small that it's hardly even a novel at all'. One bloke remarked in a classic backhander that he liked me and Frank Moorhouse because neither of us was any good at writing novels.

―――

A hard-faced, blue-eyed poet in a singlet and jeans gave me tips on how to teach writing in Pentridge: 'Take a packet of Camel. Camel plain. Chuck 'em on the table and say, "Help yourselves."'

―――

I was the only woman writer at the dinner. As the evening progressed I felt the foreign writers' egos balloon and take up even more air than did the pall of cigar smoke that issued thickly from their lips. Everybody deferred to the French *nouveau romancier*. He was actually rather pleasant. The Cuban big-shot avoided meeting my eye at all. I sneaked away into the garden after dessert. His glamorous wife, also Cuban, came out and sat beside me in the dark. I asked her, 'What is your work?' She looked at me with a blank surprise. 'I don' *work*. I maarried to berry fah-mous wriiiter.'

―――

The ravaged beauty takes me to her newly renovated pied-à-terre close to the city. We drink tea and coffee. She is charming in the way that women (especially beauties) of her age and class can be: 'How *dreadful*! That must have been *ab*solutely *dev*astating!' etc—those phrases of the consummate listener, women's expressions that mean simply, 'I am paying attention to your tale', but which probably serve, as well, to conceal boredom and the fact that she is thinking of something else, something private, paying attention to her own silent story.

―――

I was taken to visit a high school. Some students read out their stories. I loved this and was able to show it. Afterwards their teacher and I laughed happily together about the frequent theme of shit. One girl's story was even entitled *The Droppings*.

At 4 am someone opened my door and walked in. Waking in the dark, I thought, 'Oh no—I must have gone to sleep in somebody else's room by accident.'

'W-who's there?'

'Security. I can smell smoke. Is everything all right?'

'It must be my mosquito coil.'

'Sorry! Goodnight.'

When my heart stopped thumping I thought, 'Well, at least somebody's looking after me, even if I don't know who he is and will never see him again.'

In the long-term carpark at Tullamarine, waiting for the bus, sitting on an old hunk of timber against a cyclone-wire fence through which the morning sun is carefully warming my back. Birds. A phone ringing in the Budget office. Cars close and distant. Men's voices shouting, a hose squirting air. A small, cool breeze. A smell of grass.

My little niece gives me, Christmas-wrapped, a beautiful seaside stone, exactly the size to fit the palm.

After a warm night: rosy sky; remaining darkness clustering inside trees; pale objects drawing the new light towards them.

A party for Laurie Anderson in a beautiful gallery in the Domain. Arty people: some whose gender was not immediately apparent, others wearing exaggerated outfits—one bloke in a kind of helmet with shiny metal objects attached to it.

The biographer is going to AA. She told me she realised she had spent a lot of her life feeling envious and jealous, but censoring these emotions and denying to herself that she felt them. And I remembered—but did not speak about it, for she seemed to need to be the one doing the talking, though I could see that it was tiring her—a day when she came to my house, sat down opposite me at the table, and said, in her determined, dangerously smiling way that used to make me shiver at what she was about to hit me with, 'I've noticed that you use the word "envious" a great deal more than anyone I know.'

I wonder if I will ever meet a man I can love. Love, let alone live with. At my age is this such a tall order? Yes, it is. In a shop window I saw a poster of a naked man in profile holding a naked baby. The photo was cropped at the point of the man's torso where his cock began to be visible: I saw with a shock the stiff little bush of pubic hair. I had forgotten that such intimate sights existed. If I'm not careful I will forget my own body, too. Well—I may be lonely, but at least I'm not bored, and neither am I being hated by someone who is supposed to be loving me.

The movie I wrote is going to Cannes. Fear of the pincer action: on one side, public attention, on the other, the rage of people who see themselves portrayed.

In the Botanic Gardens A and I lie on two blankets that he's spread on the Oak Lawn and read *The Europeans* aloud. The bliss of being read to. The speckled shade, small children shouting and running across the grass. We take it in turns, chapter by chapter. The long sentences tax our powers of forward-seeing, but our skills develop as we warm to it. My crabby temper evaporates in the beautiful autumn day. The leaves are hardly brown, let alone on the ground.

The ex-junkie borrowed $68 off me ten days ago and has not been seen since. I thought I'd wait another week before I made inquiries. Then he called.

'Sorry I haven't paid back the money you lent me.'
Silence.
'But I—umm—well, I need to borrow some more. I need $80.'
Pause.
'No. I don't want to lend it to you.'
Pause.
'I'm crook and I need to go to work.'
'No. I don't want to lend you any money.'
'Oh. All right.'
'OK?'
'Yeah. Bye.'

So the gossip is true. I didn't hesitate, or feel guilty, or even give a reason. I must be making progress.

———

Cool, cloudy day at Anglesea. They took us for a swim. Everyone was leaving the beach for lunch and it started to rain lightly. The water was green and the sky was grey. Big, cold, slow swells that didn't break. P turned blue: 'My teeth are what you call chattering!' After five minutes it was no longer cold. We were all laughing and shouting—blasts of intense joy. On the way back to the house I looked around me at the low scrub and the greyish air and the massed tea-tree in a sort of bliss.

———

A movie about war crimes in Poland. A small crowd had gathered to watch the exhumation of bodies from a mass grave. Two men at the very edge of the trench slipped on the crumbling soil and fell in among the blackened, rotting remains. Their frantic scrambling to get out was frightful.

I thought my ladder had been stolen, but it turns out F had come over and taken it. What is the actual *process* by which one separates oneself from another person?

I bought a cassette of Maria Callas and played it in the car. When she sang *Io son' l'umile ancella* I amazed myself by bursting out sobbing. Not just a few tears but real weeping. All kinds of good and comforting thoughts rushed through my head. *I* want to be 'the humble servant-maid'.

I dreamt that someone threw blood on my long skirt. I took it off and wrapped myself in a towel while I washed out the blood. A young Eastern European man was anxious that someone would come in and suspect indiscretion. He stood in a corner with his finger across his lips. I couldn't convey to him that there was nothing to suspect. Someone was playing a piano for children to dance to.

The surgeon's wife actually considered buying a watch that cost $700. The courteous young man serving her kept his face blank while she loudly bashed my ear about Australia's descent into the maelstrom of unionism, high taxation and welfare. 'Workers are bludgers,' she said with scorn. 'Rostered days off, one a fortnight.' 'What's wrong with that?' I said, really wanting to know. She didn't have an answer.

The law student came downstairs to tell me something he'd read in a judgment he's studying. 'This judge reckons the law says that as much responsibility is to be expected of a twelve-year-old as of a twenty-one-year-old.' I noticed how white his face was, mauve shadows under his eyes. I said, 'Do you feel sick? You've gone very pale.' 'No—it's just the shock of the judgment.' His emotions often show in the colour of his face. When his girlfriend was coming back from overseas his skin was green.

―――

The prisoners in the Pentridge writing group liked gasbagging about families, about touching people while you're talking, and whether this habit came from your parents. One bloke said, 'My family's very close, always huggin' and that. When my mum comes in here she throws her arms round me and starts bawlin'. I could've started meself—but *you* know—you have to—' He mimes himself darting embarrassed, tiny glances to left and right. Imagine if everybody in Pentridge started bawling at once, screws and all. The tears would rise up and spill over the curved top of the bluestone walls.

―――

We walked out to Princes Park to look for the comet. A found it and I saw it, very blurred, six times as big as a star, like a headlight in a very thick fog.

―――

Walked to the shop. Picked a twig of bottlebrush with three flowers on it. Looked at it with extreme pleasure. At home I noticed a shifting and saw that a praying mantis was hiding among its spiky leaves. 'Poor thing. Poor thing.' I took it out the front and held the twig against the wisteria: it stepped across and, adjusting its camouflage, disappeared.

―――

M read me some Banjo Paterson poems. 'Where the breezes shake the grass.'

―――

Peggy Glanville-Hicks was interviewed on TV.

'You love it, don't you—music?' said the interviewer, in a shy, humble voice.

'Well,' said the old woman, holding a whining black poodle in her arms, 'it's international. It can go anywhere. It doesn't need translation. And its manifestation is the displacement of air.'

———

Once I accepted F's analysis, in his letter—that we'd never really committed ourselves to each other as married people do—all my victim feelings and anger fell away. All that was left was a terrible sadness. Days of crying at the slightest stimulus.

———

'Afterwards she repented it bitterly, but she was hopeless at apologising: instead of retracting her feelings, what she always did was to say that she was sorry for expressing them, a kind of amends that costs nothing and carries the built-in rebuke that the other person is unable to bear the truth.' —Penelope Gilliatt, 'The Redhead', in *The Transatlantic Review*

———

Sick in bed. My sister came round and told me the latest family gossip. We laughed and laughed. I thought of a little movie about how information passes round a family—very sternly structured, solely in the form of two-way conversations—all in dialogue, clothes and body language. 'And I said, "*Look*, Mum, there are dead letters in dead letter offices all over the *world*."' When I get better from this I'm gonna WORK. I'm going to make fur and feathers fly, I'm gonna ATTACK IDEAS and *let the chips fall where they may.*

———

If I had a little boy I'd call him Angelo.

———

'What I missed,' said the law student about the time his girlfriend was away, 'wasn't so much getting love as giving it. I just wanted to—I wanted to cover her with love.'

———

A said that anger ruled my life. Which of course made me furious but I tried not to be. Once again his humility and ability to accept criticism took away my weapons. He was washing up while we talked. When he got to the saucepan he turned aside and left it lying in the water. All the while, as the talk went to and fro, I was looking at the saucepan in the water, congealing with fat, bobbing in the sink, and I was thinking, 'Can't you finish a job? *That's* what makes me angry with you. You're sloppy.'

———

Dreamt I was doing an English exam and making a mess of it. I had missed one of the essay questions. I panicked, and began to give up. I looked out the window. A bird flew away. I felt sad and hopeless, as if all were lost. A woman supervisor looked at me through a grille. Suddenly I laughed and said, 'I'm a famous novelist! I don't *need* this exam!' She laughed too but still I felt ashamed, as if a necessary step were missing in my self-preparation for life.

———

A horrible nuclear disaster, a meltdown, at Chernobyl in the Ukraine. Nobody knows how many people have died.

———

Dinner with the famous ones. Among men, as usual, I became aware that I have no subject on which I can deliver quantities of information, facts etc. Savage gossip. I wondered how many knives would be quivering in my back after the door had closed.

———

All day at the Royal Women's birthing centre. I longed to watch a birth but of course this was out of the question, though I did glimpse, through opening doors, several cunts—one bloody, with a doctor sitting at it sewing it up. A huge placenta in a metal dish, the young nurses examining it bloody to the wrists. The matter-of-fact calm of midwives. The premature babies, their shuddering and gasping, their appalling tininess, I wanted to sob out loud. As if a nose were not made for anything but to have a tube shoved up it.

―――――

The nurse's husband, in a letter: 'Geez you women cry a lot but yer as tough as nails. I walk around feeling limp and inferior in the face of that iron-hearted sex you belong to.'

―――――

I drove her to school at 7 am for camp. We laughed all the way at I have forgotten what. She's had a dramatic, rather sixties haircut. 'It makes you look older,' I said. 'At least eighteen.' Her face burst into a joyful smile. I love her as one is afraid to love, through superstition. Even having written that…

―――――

A letter from the American. 'I swim beside you in spirit.'

―――――

Dreamt I was to be ordained and to give the sacrament. Anxious because I hadn't studied the liturgy. I woke thinking that if I were ordained I would be qualified to bury the dead. And the part I want to lay to rest is the girl I was in the 1960s. Who thought she was free but who was in fact chained. Who had two abortions and was not loved or respected by the men she slept with, although she believed she was, through inability to see the facts and insufficient imagination about what went on in men's minds and hearts. Cruel to herself without realising it.

―――――

Two people told me they'd seen me on TV. The man said, 'You looked sad.' The woman said, 'Your eyes were twinkling, as if you were about to laugh.'

I suppose being sad and laughing are not mutually exclusive.

―――――

The psychotherapist talks about 'men in suits' who come to him.

'They think they can hand me their problem and get me to fix it for them. They're so blocked. It's sad.'

'They must be terribly lonely?'

'And frightened. At some stage they always cry.'

Up at Primrose Gully with Y. We're both scared of snakes. And we're ignorant of electricity, and how to use the car battery for power in the house. The neighbour from down the road: plain, with a mouth that's drawn in, watery eyes, filthy farmer's clothes, a loud, rather harsh voice—but a lively mind, witty turn of phrase, a tough and cheerful friendliness. He called each of us by name once or twice, as if to fix us in his mind. He offered to help with buying a chainsaw. I liked him very much, and felt lucky to have met him. He mentioned in passing that one of their children had died.

Dreamt I was to sleep in a borrowed room. I asked the woman, 'What's in that drawer?' 'Maps,' she said. I looked at her with happy respect, knowing that she was a traveller, someone who'd been to strange, distant and perhaps dangerous places and who had returned. She seemed a calm person, the kind who makes plans and fulfils them with steady application.

A hawk on a tree. We saw its shoulders.

I *dread* having to *become a Christian.*

A beautiful letter came from J. He said he loved my work, and that though I may not define goodness as he does, I was 'searching for a language of grace'. I went stumbling out on to the footpath still reading, and when I glanced down, the pebbles sprang into such bright relief that I had to look again. I had the dog with me and we walked slowly round the big block. It was a windy, sparkling afternoon.

———

'People who can't accept a gift,' said the Jungian, 'often feel a need to wound the giver.'

———

The biographer does that maddening thing of asking, 'Am I boring you?' at the exact moment when I am most deeply attentive to what she is saying: thus she breaks my concentration. It's as if she's jealous of her own discourse: when I'm paying total attention to *it*, she needs to force on me the distinction between *what she is saying* and *her*.

———

A Giuseppe Bertolucci movie, *Segreti Segreti*. I was struck dumb by its sophisticated structure and the deep sense of the society it emerges from. The final scene, where the terrorist sits opposite the woman judge and begins to reel off the names of her comrades, made me want to get down on my knees and grovel. Why can't Australian films achieve that density? It must be because our society is so porous.

———

At Primrose Gully the grass is stiff with frost. Feet aching with cold. The clear patch on the window where I wiped it to see out has refrozen in prettier patterns.

———

I saw a big fat koala fall out of a tree. It sloped off towards the road with a sulky look over its shoulder. I laughed out loud and clapped my hands but it paid me no attention. Its victorious rival, clinging to a tall slender trunk, had what looked like a bloody wound on its chest. Life is carnage up here.

———

Census night. The law student and I were filling out the form. He had to say what he was in relation to the head of the household. I expected him to write 'tenant' but he put 'friend'. I think of this on and off all day and it comforts me.

———

Hannah and Her Sisters. Too close to the bone. Oh, it hurts so much to look back. I rode over him roughshod. Impatient, vain, self-important, and then abject. No wonder he can't stand me. I can hardly stand myself.

———

House full of music. The law student and his huge friend roaring away upstairs on amplified bass and guitar. The girls downstairs singing Schubert at the piano.

———

The I Ching says that flight means saving oneself under any circumstances, whereas retreat is a sign of strength. Voluntary retreat. Friendly retreat. Cheerful retreat. That's what I'm after.

———

As the afternoon was ending my friends took me for a walk along the Glebe waterfront. The sky was quite black in parts, then streaked, swirled and plumed like a Turner painting. A strong, warm wind blew. The evening star shone steadily between rents in the cloth. 'Australians are hopeless with land use,' said the Cretan. 'In Europe there'd be a couple of little restaurants along here.' He showed me some photos he'd taken of me last year and I was shocked by my ugliness: spotted skin, lined face, ugly haircut, dark expressions. I mean I was *shocked*. I quailed at the possibility that I will be alone now for the rest of my life. That I will never turn back into a womanly being but will find myself stuck here in between, plain and dry in my manly or boyish little clothes. I was afraid of my ugliness. I thought, I will go on getting older. This is not a temporary phase. I am moving slowly and surely on towards decrepitude. But walking with them I became happy. I picked wattle, bottlebrush, Geraldton wax. The Cretan poured out so much botanical information that we teased him and called him Professor. They asked me if I would ever consider moving to Sydney. 'I feel,' said the Cretan, 'that you're on the verge of plunging into a pool of clear water.'

Up here, among kind friends, I forget my troubles.

———

How the nun says goodbye: 'Go in peace.' 'You too,' I say, without having to think. Afterwards I felt her little blessing and was grateful.

———

F says I ought to get a regular job, so as to be less 'frantic'.
   'What could I be?'
   'A teacher. A publisher's reader.'

———

The historian who came to my reading at Monash. She told a little anecdote, with gestures, about using the expression 'phallische Symbolen' to some visiting German friends of her age: to her astonishment they had never heard the term. She was speaking about a row of carrots standing on a shelf in a juice shop.

———

I like it when my sister talks about nursing. She told me about nasogastric tubes and how to insert them. And about colonic irrigations.

———

Les Murray's wonderful poem 'When Bounty Is Down to Persimmons and Lemons'. The infuriating accuracy and simplicity of his images—birds that 'trickle down through' foliage. *Of course*, I think, that is what they *do*—why didn't *I* know how to say it? '*Women's Weekly* summer fashions in the compost turn blue.'

———

Evil Angels—its marvellous combination of tenderness for the characters with an awesome ability to handle masses of factual material. And the delicacy of its emotional texture. The whole thing is buzzing with life.

———

At the school concert a girl's proud father says, 'I *love* you!' and squeezes her in his arms. She shrieks, '*Ewww*, YUCK!' and fights to break free. He grips tighter with a demonic grin.

———

To the dentist for a crown preparation. He stuck the needle twice into my lip, babbling rapidly, '*Oooh*, yes you're a good girl a brave girl a very very good girl a brave girl.' Almost two hours of grinding, drilling, injections, string, blood, impression taken twice, post screwed in. As the time went on I became weakened by attrition. His waggish, chatty spiel, his way of addressing me as if I were a child and stroking my face while the impression set, caused a regression which reached its peak when I told him, after he'd cemented the temporary crown on, that it felt big in my mouth. He snapped at me: 'I *asked* you before! And you *said* it wasn't touching!' To my horror I burst into tears. 'I'm sorry! I'm so tired! I didn't understand exactly what you were asking—oh, boo hoo!' He was astonished, and embarrassed: 'WHY are you so tired?' 'I've had my mouth wide open for TWO HOURS!' He put me back in the chair and drilled off a bit more. I tried hard to control myself, for fear that if I jerked he would puncture my already bloody gum, but I couldn't stop my quivering sobs, like a child's, and tears ran off my face. He and the nurse acted soberly. The nurse didn't look at me again. It was awful. His falsely cheery goodbye. I stumbled off down the hallway. Before I reached the street I had recognised it: Dad territory. His baby talk had lulled me, and then the shock of his anger—a sudden withdrawal of approval. At the traffic lights I met Mum's brother. He didn't even notice I was crying, so I quickly stopped.

I lie in bed thinking voluptuously of the stories I'm going to write.

'I think,' says R, 'that people who "long to have children" are just being romantic.'

The bloke next door shows me the room with bunks that he says his children will sleep in, if he ever finds anyone to have them with. I forbear to point out that any child who sat up in the top bunk would be beheaded by the ceiling fan.

The plane lurched in the air and was lit by lightning, but in Melbourne the land was sunlit and the air was crisp.

I entered the living room and found Mum sitting alone on the couch, looking elegant. During our short conversation I had one of those moments of disconnection from myself: looking at her face I felt strongly that I both knew and did not know this person.

The high-school drama night. M's house did Molière, *Le Médecin malgré lui*, which she had directed. It ripped along, seductive, hilarious. Her fleeting bit-part as the passing stranger who tries to stop Sganarelle from beating his wife—she was a flash of lightning, her face white with righteous anger and then with alarm and apology—people shouted with laughter. This skinny little trouper of mine. Not mine much longer.

Raymond Carver called collect when I wasn't home, and the law student, confused, caused him to hang up.

Out near the rubbish bins I ask my neighbour if she knows anything about Melanie Klein. 'I absolutely *detest* psychoanalysis,' she snaps. I bet you do. Look at your life.

A woman reviews my postcards book in *Meanjin*. Covers it with praise. 'Artful.' 'This brilliant story.' 'Consistently good.' 'Outstanding.' I'm glowing, defences down. Then on her way out she flicks me with her tail: 'She is at her best, so far, when dealing with…middle-class, contemporary living and relationships. This is her great talent. It remains to be seen whether this is also her limitation.' What do they WANT from me?

Visconti's wonderful movie *Bellissima*. We writhed with laughter in our seats: the comedy of the child's suffering. How there's often a secondary activity in the background of the main action: a line of tiny distant dancers rehearsing on an outdoor stage: '*Uno! Due! Tre! Quattro!*' A man on a high scaffold banging in a nail with tremendous arm movements. Layer after layer of life.

Afterwards at the Rialto A ordered another beer when everyone else was ready to go home. Three quarters of the way down it he went off to the lavatory. T seized his glass and swigged a large mouthful, to speed up his painful slowness. 'Here he comes,' she hissed. 'Is there foam on my lips?'

I want to write a story called 'The Punishment for Not Being Beautiful'.

I shot off a whole roll of colour film in our house while everyone was out. First I took one of each bed as it had been left; then I crammed myself into corners, set things up, crouched, stood on chairs, screwing up my face, framing things—to take photos you must have to relearn to *look*. Filled with respect for people who do this difficult thing beautifully. I loved trying. Thought of writing a story with no characters in it, called 'Four Beds', and even began it, but put it aside, out of fear I suppose.

At their house we ate barbecued chicken out of a paper bag and listened to Nat King Cole.

Dreamt I was a teacher and there was one uncontrollable boy in my class. I sent him to the principal. I said, 'I'm not stupid, you know, no matter how much you dislike me. What *do* you think of me?' He replied frankly, 'I think you're *awful*.' At that moment I saw a close-up, near my face, of a bush covered in pretty little flowers, in the front garden of our old house at Ocean Grove.

Outside the post office the dog shat out a tapeworm. It trailed behind her and I had to put my foot on it to snap it off.

In Readings I picked up a novel about a sadomasochistic affair. I read it in furtive bursts, in case someone looked over my shoulder. It was frightening. I realised I am very much a moralist: afraid of the tremendous power of sex when it's let loose from love and social restraints.

'There are people,' a reader writes to me reproachfully, 'who have their babies at home, get married with flair, and get buried in triumph.'

After the funding meeting comes a surprising letter from the old poet who worked with us, a small, gentle, mildly spoken, slightly trembling woman with long white hair in a French roll: 'You will never be in need of friends. I mean of all sorts and degrees—and whatever your own personal uncertainties may be.' The extraordinary kindness of this. She mothered me. I'm not used to it.

———

Spring comes. People fall in love—or they will, when the sunny breezes blow and exams are soon and cafe tables are put out on the pavements. Will I? I can't imagine who with.

———

On a sparkling morning, windows wide open, Crowded House on the stereo, the law student and I wrestle with a lamb shank. He twists and wrenches with the rubber gloves on, I hack with a big blunt knife, so he can make stock and cook us some soup. Carnage over the trough. Blood splatters his front. 'Take your shirt off and soak it.' 'I wouldn't have known about doing that.' 'Women know a lot about blood.' He's the closest I'll ever get to having a son.

———

Primrose Gully with T. There's a star beside the moon that neither of us has ever noticed before. Star and moon are both reflected in the dam so vividly that it's unnerving—as if we were suddenly seeing everything upside down.

———

A big dry wind roars all night. Stars brilliant. Several are yellow. 'Look at them,' says T. 'Aren't they queer. They make the others look really *blue*. They look like electric bulbs.' She messed around with some grass and rags and came up what she called a 'pagan bride', a little straw doll in a dirty cloth dress and hood. She called me to look at it and I got a funny feeling, seeing it leaning against a small bush. It looked primitive, mysterious and powerful. Maybe I could write about A's panic when I said I was going to get my palm read. His refusal to tell me his astrological sign. Can I use the Cathedral Tearooms? The women's ordination?

Ayers Rock? It could be a novel. Oh, calm down.

―――

I sat at the table working away with the Faber Castells while the law student played his Jazz Originals book on the piano. Drawing beats colouring-in hands down.

―――

In a magazine a sketch of three women sitting at a table, and on it, in the foreground, a crudely drawn pistol and a very high-heeled shoe. The artist does people with hardly any lines: women with funny little bobbed haircuts and sober faces.

―――

'I saw how beautiful she was,' said the bridegroom in his speech, 'and I saw that a man'd be a fool not to want to share his life with her.'

―――

The things men say to me sometimes at public gatherings. In a strange, jesting, almost pugnacious tone they say that they like my work, and then they tell me what bugs them about it. This one couldn't stand the way I 'talk about Bach and popular music in the same breath. That's an *abomination* to me.'

―――

They must have seven kids by now, the youngest only a few months old. Felt a longing to visit them, to see them all thronging, hear their family language and songs, jokes at the table, the *noise* of it.

―――

The academic was wearing a little pale satin shift to mid-calf, like a pretty nightie. Watched her in the line for food, saw how large her head looked, pale and tired, well-set on her slimmed-down body.

―――

Should the law student write his new almost-girlfriend a letter? If so, what sort? My tactician's idea: a postcard. What'll he write on it, though? Something short. What about 'Dear X, Come back quick. Love—' and sign? Perfect! But should he put some kisses? Just put one. OK—he doesn't want to be *heavy*.

———

Dream of a court case. A report typed on a typewriter that made small plants grow out of the page. I had to push the little stalks and leaves gently aside so I could read the print at their roots.

———

A visitor from Circus Oz. Her grey hair, flamboyant comfortable clothes. In the kitchen we talked with urgency and uttered screams of laughter.

———

My mind is full of stories but I lack the nerve to catch one and try to pin it down.

———

After the concert of mediaeval music the academic said she had seen the counter-tenor walking down the street with his little drum over his shoulder on a leather strap. We thought that he probably slept under a hedge.

———

We quarrelled. M spoke sharply to me. I suppose I was being silly and middle-aged. I was embarrassed that her rebuke had hurt me. She gave me a perfunctory hug which I accepted. I drove off to review a play, alone in my car and my clip-on earrings. Walking in the dark down Queensberry Street I felt quite desperate. I thought, 'This far down is when you ought to pray.' I didn't know how, but the thought presented itself like a reminder of a *practical technique*.

———

A thunderbolt struck me—*a character*. Ideas and plans flooded in and out of my mind all day. Such a richness of material that I hardly dare to look straight at it: I have to keep looking in the other direction. Surges of excitement and confidence, which suddenly ebb away and leave me panicking: *can I do this? Can I find out what I need to know?* By this I mean that a creature is beginning to exist which will lead me into a story. All I had to do was wait for my guide. I stepped out the back gate, my head bursting with this, and remembered that state where one lives night and day in the world of the novel and one is NOT AVAILABLE. No wonder men don't stick around.

A Russian cruise liner crashes into a tanker and sinks in 'the warm waters of the Baltic Sea'. Three hundred die. 'Those who had retired for the night would have had little chance of escape.'

Dreamt I cooked a meal and put those green anti-slug pellets in it. We all ate it before the terrible truth was revealed; and yet we agreed that its flavour had been delicious, with a hindsight tinge of horror.

A spiteful review of a friend's novel. I ask the magazine editor what the critic looks like. 'Oh,' he says, 'she's one of those Australian women with thin faces and black hair who remind you of Heckle and Jeckle.'

Primrose Gully. My sister comes down the track from the car, all in black, sunglasses, white-faced, like a refugee. Very upset and weeping. The married man she's having an affair with, his coldness in public, his failure to turn up, she lay awake all night waiting. Disgusting memories of my own. I talked at length about humiliation, low self-esteem, self-punishment etc. I must learn to shut up. Talking loosely and inefficiently is an indulgence. We went for a walk to look at the river, and back across the gully under the big pine tree. We picked up firewood. In the morning she said, 'I woke up once in the night and looked out the window.

The sky was full of stars. I thought I must be in heaven.'

———

Against Z's back door jamb, after the *Rigoletto* rehearsal, leaned a small, white-faced, long-headed, warped figure. Weird, like something that had crept out of a dark hole where it had been lying for a long time in a tense and twisted position. 'This is V,' said Z. When the others went out of the room I felt nervous, like a schoolgirl having to entertain a grown-up. As we walked away from the house R said, 'Just as well neither of us is married to *him*!'

———

Later, a dream: some kind of dark, dumb attraction between V and me.

———

My sister breaks it off with the guy. 'I felt really happy for two days, and I still feel good. But sometimes I get very *sad*.'

'Sadness is better than wretchedness though, isn't it. It's more dignified.'

I felt very proud of her. As if she'd dragged herself out of a swamp in front of my very eyes.

———

We walked the dog round Princes Park and kept noticing a strong smell of animal shit. We inspected our boot soles—nothing. 'It must be a circus,' said A, meaning it as a joke, but then I remembered that there *is* a circus on the other side of the footy ground—I saw the two camels, tall and lonely away from their desert.

———

A doco about Berlin after the war. Footage of a boy of eight or so picking his way across a huge pile of building rubble, cap on head, pack on back, bare knees, boots—answering the questions of a disembodied voice: 'Where are you going?' 'I've lost my family. I'm looking for them.' 'How long since you saw them?' 'Six weeks. Goodbye!' He smiles, turns and walks away, a man with a mission—then a few yards further on turns again, waves, calls out 'Goodbye!' and goes on his way. I stood at the sink dumbly washing and stacking, despairing of ever having anything worth saying. I know nothing of what is savage and cruel in life. My work is as ignorant as I am. *I don't know anything.* But maybe it's the devil talking when we get the idea that someone who knows no savagery knows nothing—as if only evil were real and the rest weightless.

———

Near us, after midnight in the piano bar, sat an old man with a carnation in his buttonhole. He clapped his square hands in time to the music in such a way as to let it be known that he was with the band. Behind us a woman knocked over a stemmed glass. It smashed. She moved off to the dance floor without a backward look. A Japanese tourist at a third table bent down, picked up the glass, stem and base from the carpet, and placed them reverently on the glass-smasher's table. The only person who observed the Japanese woman's act, and her low bow, was a half-drunken young man, the gooseberry left at the dropper's table: he stared at her, loafing back in his chair, and made no sign.

———

The worst moment at the funding meeting was rejecting the application of a man who wanted to write a novel about the Kampuchean bloodbath. I looked at his file and thought, This guy's seen people suffocated in plastic bags and I'm sitting here telling him he can't have money to tell his story. I tried to make a coherent statement but felt heavy and desperate. I wanted to say that our procedures were inadequate and frustrating, but all that came out was, in a dull voice, 'He used to be a journalist and now he's a labourer.' 'It's a tough world,' said the chair, and on we went.

———

'He became a Roman Catholic after his son died of a drug overdose,' said the journalist. 'Course, being a Catholic in the right wing of the Labor Party isn't exactly a disadvantage…'

―――

L, an unfairly handsome guy who was at the festival. I like him more than I'd expected to. Rather soft, talkative, an enthusiast, the sort of person who gives your forearm a little push as he approaches the punch-line of his story. I suspect a series of terrific emotional crashes in his past. Why does a man like this attract me? Don't be silly. Because he's *gorgeous*.

―――

The student asked me if I thought love could connect people across boundaries of class. 'Of course.' He said he'd been convinced by Communism, then felt its rigidity: 'It dropped off me like a shell.'

―――

At lunchtime I sat in the gallery beside a large, flat, shallow body of water in a pebble-bottomed bed. It quivered like the water in my best dream: trembled with inner life. A girl beside me on the couch, wearing modern clothes, was deep in a serious paperback novel. I sat there and thought, *I am happy*.

―――

Fay Zwicky on the effect of Les Murray's work: 'Why then, after wrestling long and hard with many poems in this book, have I come away feeling excluded, mystified and defeated?' *Excluded* is the word I had been using.

―――

My sister got some freebies to Mondo Rock. In the hour of waiting she took us to a new place called the Hyatt on Collins. A noisy palace in pink marble. A very amateurish singer and pianist, both boys, murdered certain innocent classics. '*Tsk*,' she said, tossing back a glass of terrible Australian champagne. 'That's a very pedestrian version of "Walk On By".' Next morning the law student sneered but I thought Mondo Rock were quite good. During one old-fashioned guitar solo I found I had tears in my eyes. I thought, I've been lonely for a year. I can still *like* this music. I will spend the summer dancing. I will have fun.

———

A house I like. Full of light. A backyard full of bull-dozable sheds. A huge park in front, and behind, a view over to Mount Macedon. Do people like me buy houses?

———

V's proprietary tone when he speaks of the high priests of European literature—'Yes, they are peculiar titles,' he says about Canetti's autobiography—reminds me of the German poet who boasted to me about how he had once sat up all night reading Chekhov's letters. As if no one else had ever done this.

———

The movie I wrote was screened on TV. I felt a waning of enthusiasm in the room as it progressed. All I saw were its faults and crudities—points at which it was rushed—big, far-off images instead of the small, intimate ones I had wanted. I felt tired, foolish, somehow ashamed. When it was over I hoped someone might ring me, but O, who was staying the night, went straight to the phone and made shouting interstate calls for an hour. I was too deflated to object. Then, very late, the old woman in Queensland who likes my work rang and said, 'I know I'm biased but I loved it. I cried.' I heard the sweetness in her voice and thought, She has been a pretty woman.

———

At the dinner table the law student's eyelids kept falling. He had plainly been at the pub all afternoon. The dainty Japanese backpacker looked at him carefully and said, 'Have you been drinking? Because there is strong smer of arcohor.'

L shows me a list he's typed up, of adjectives and epithets used by reviewers about his novel. An A4 page and a half. He read it out to me and we laughed and laughed. The whole range, from 'meaningless and pretentious' to 'brilliant', was covered.

Woken pleasantly from a nap by Bach on the piano downstairs, those powerful patterns flexing their muscles through the afternoon when no one's home but me and my daughter.

'I always thought that when we accepted things they overpowered us…This turns out not to be true at all, and it is only by accepting them that one can assume an attitude towards them.' From a letter by one of Jung's patients. —Peter O'Connor in *Understanding Jung*

Girls pass in the street, clapping a fast rhythm and singing a vigorous song.

In the pub after Carlton lost the Grand Final, the table of roaring, bellowing brothers. 'This is going to be one of those *nights*,' I muttered to one of their young wives, 'and I'm fucked if I'm going to put up with it.' She laughed in a comradely way and said, 'Aren't they terrible!' How come these yobs all end up with fabulous women?

V wrote, 'I wanted to see you again straight away.' So I was not imagining it. A gong of terror sounded in the bottom of my stomach. Something chilling in him. His intellect.

While I was asleep the Japanese girl got stranded in North Melbourne at 2.30 am and called our place for help. The Sydney visitor answered, told her he couldn't do anything for her and she should call a taxi—leaves her to her fate in the dark. She gives up and sleeps at the Youth Hostel. I know nothing of this till eight in the morning when she calls me. Furious and ashamed I drive over and collect her. When the law student hears that she had thought the rude visitor was him, he is strangled with distress: 'If it'd been me I'd've *run* to North Melbourne. I'd've piggybacked her.' 'I know you would, you darling,' I say fondly. 'Oh *yuck*,' says M with a grimace.

―――

I walk down the street in bright lipstick and light-coloured clothes. People look into my face and smile. I've got seven-league boots on. I'm alive again.

―――

Bulletin review of our movie. So splenetic it's embarrassing: apparently all my characters, in everything I ever write, are 'renowned for their unlikeableness', and the director has taken cinema back to a primitive stage before cameras could move. 'If Ms Campion is to be hailed as the new empress of Australian film…' Wonder what made *him* so crabby.

―――

'Your daughter's terrifically striking-looking, isn't she,' says L. 'Boys must be swarming round her, I suppose.'

'Well, not really. She knocks around with a rather blue-stocking crowd. They repel boys with contemptuous stares.'

―――

At the party a clean and bright young man in a striped shirt and little round tortoiseshell spectacles, with a flamboyantly Hungarian name, told me he'd read only one of my books and thought I ought to 'broaden my range' and 'write about the proletariat'. I was a bit drunk and said, 'What bullshit. *Why?*'

'Because the middle class is boring. It's narrow, small, confined, a minority.'

His wife or girlfriend, a striking dark woman, said, '*I'm* from "the proletariat". He's got a thing about it.' She looked at me in a friendly way and laughed. I wandered off, shaken by his challenge.

Rain is falling softly and steadily. This is comforting. What do I need comfort for? Being a member of the middle class. Not writing. Being forty-three and three-quarters. Being a solitary woman. Only no. 2 is a painful thing. All the rest often give me extreme pleasure.

Constant struggle between money and time: will I waste an hour going into town to Bell's Discounts to get the skin cream cheap, or will I waste a couple of extra dollars at the corner chemist and save the hour?

L hasn't answered my letter. The sense of having lost something, that his silence provokes. Remember that always, when a horror balloons in my memory around something I've written, a calm re-examination of the thing itself reveals a lightness of tone that saves it from being the crusher I have let myself imagine. Do my duties, try to get more sleep, drink less, try to keep this feeling of *worth* alive.

The American poet at the festival dinner meets my eye from the opposite corner of the long table and *holds it*, almost aggressively, with a small smile on his very wide, very smooth face. He holds my gaze for such a long time, smiling like a little brown Buddha, that I laugh out loud in a spasm of embarrassment. Later, I move to his end of the table, where a woman is declaring that feminism has caused an increase in male homosexuality. The poet says he thinks most people are sexually 'much more timid' than our society allows them to be. A bunch of us talk for a long time about sex and love. The young editor says he has never slept with anyone he hasn't 'got to know really well first'. The poet says he's always felt he was 'just as eager for love as women are supposed to be'; that he has 'never been interested in sex without love'. I opine that people organise their emotions to accord with their sexual interests, 'so that what you get is emotional rather than sexual promiscuity'. 'Love,' says the young editor, 'just *comes*.' 'Does that mean,' I ask, 'that you can't seek it, then?'

———

I am the only person in the world who carries round an inventory of my crimes. Everyone else is busy with their own.

———

The poet comes up to me in the lobby and says, 'I get consolation from seeing your face.'

———

Today I'll get up, have a shower, see how my period's going; make my bed; wear something clean and comfortable; go to the last day of the festival; maybe walk across the river and look at the water; and come home.

———

Mum comes to stay a night. I'm so tired. I ask her if she'll 'look after me'.

'Is there anything in the kitchen?' she asks. 'Any…eggs?'

'The trouble is, Mum, I haven't been here for days. There's no food.'

'I'll go to the shop.'

'Do you know what I'd really like? Chicken noodle soup out of a packet, and a boiled egg, and some fingers of toast.'

She laughs and looks pleased. The law student is playing 'My Funny Valentine' on the piano. My sister calls to tell me she's met Cyndi Lauper at a party: 'She's just a regular woman. She's *great*.' I go upstairs and lie down.

Mum returns. She brings my meal upstairs, sits on my bed and chats to me. I lie here bathing in her wandering tales. Sometimes my eyes close, but I don't have any trouble staying awake. I feel loving and thankful towards her. She kisses me goodnight at nine o'clock and goes downstairs with my tray. On my way to the bathroom I glance into the mirror. My face is young and smooth, exactly as it was after my crack-up two years ago when I dropped my bundle and slept for twenty-four hours.

———

One of these days I'll meet a man to whom I'll be circumstantially free to say, 'Do you want to get in the car with me and drive to Darwin?' and he'll say, 'Yes,' and we'll do it.

———

The poet Rosa Cappiello. Her terrifying sadness. Her clumsy questions: 'Helen, are you happy?' and statements: 'I want someone who is clean inside.' She asks me to read out her paper, for the panel 'Why I Write'. It's full of her awkward passion. Her poems terrify me too—I read the translations for her, trying to be only a vessel or a conduit for the rage and disgust that's in them: 'Lie down, man'—wanting to ravish, to 'breathe into his lap' a sexual fury that would set the world of gender right—but I felt very Presbyterian—restrained, small, neat, quiet. One of the poems was simply too much for me and I didn't even attempt it. But the American poet took her aside and spoke to her urgently in a low voice. I heard him as I passed: 'You are really, really good. You must practise and *practise*.' She seems to have no friends, or very few, and to spend her time alone, waiting for her dole cheque. When she received her pay for the festival session she was staggered. I said, 'You must apply for a fellowship—$25,000.' She gave a strange laugh: 'I can't ask for so much money.' She is lost between Italy and here, stuck in her terrible English. She seemed a member of another species, wild, in pain, knowing things I could barely dream of—humiliations, violence, disgust, loneliness, fear. She's got a wild animal's face—although she's my age she has smooth skin, her eyes narrow and lying on high cheekbones, mouth that is generous like all Italian mouths, with a pretty top lip that doesn't move much when she speaks. Her legs are slim. Beautiful hands, small, narrow and slender; very small feet in distorting, ugly, very high-heeled sandals—her toes pinched lumps, curved in and under as if trying to hold themselves back off the pavement—squirming back to stay on the inadequate leather. 'I've suffered too much,' she said to me. 'I can't change now.' Her weak, reedy voice. When she read her poems in Italian it was barely audible. I could see her skirt quivering as she stood whispering and gabbling at the lectern.

On my way out of the Athenaeum, so tired I could hardly speak, I was approached by a young woman.

'I heard you read that story about the friend. The painter. It made me very angry. I thought it was a *cruel* story,' she said, clenching her hands. 'You took all the little illusions that people use to make life bearable, and you *stripped* and *stripped* and *stripped* them away. I'm trying to be a painter, and I—'

Exhausted, looking at her smooth pale skin, her items of silver jewellery here and there, I thought, Come back in twenty years, sweetheart, and tell me about your little illusions then.

I walk away, get into my car, drive home, and go straight to bed, at five in the afternoon. What I could have said to her was, 'Listen. *There is no comfort.* And if you think there is, then maybe you're not really an artist.'

Walking with C in the Botanic Gardens. Rain. Our shoulders were damp. We talked about our lives, our loneliness; how we are tempted to invite unwanted men back into our lives just in order to feel less alone.

———

The reason, says T, why house-hunting is so tiring: because you have to move, in fantasy, in and out of every house you look at—shift all your furniture and arrange it, and cook and eat several meals; and carry out the rubbish. Yes, and you have to *part from your daughter*, and leave your piano behind. Half of me will be with her always, longing to care for her and make a life for her.

———

Dinner at Toki with T's son. At sixteen, the pure lines of his face, those marvellous bones, the *strain* of youth in a face. His lively company, tales of bashings, school wars, 'rumbles' etc. On the way home we stop for a coffee at Notturno. A hulk with a five o'clock shadow enters, runs him through the soul handshake, and engages him in urgent conversation about someone called Eddy who is going to bash him. *'Eddy?* Oh, man.' The hulk wears a jumper with the sleeves rolled right up past his biceps. He leaves, upon being summoned by his scrawny mate outside.

'Who was *that*?'
'Hassan. He's so cool.'
'He sure is. How do you know him?'
'From school.'
'But he must be twenty-five!'
'He's the same age as me.'
'Sixteen? *Him*?'
'I bet he only shaved an hour ago. Once, he decided to grow a moustache. Next day, he had one.'

———

Spring. The curtain moves all night on fitful streams of air.

———

The house auction. My father bid for me, late, twice, and with contemptuous authority. His astonishing exhibition of cool. A merchant in his element. A life of buying and selling. 'Gawd. What a lotta mucken around. We'da bought a million dollars wortha wool by now.' My sister stood beside me uttering a stream of hard-nosed opinion and theory. I sank down on to the asphalt with my knees up and my back against the fence and stared at the ground. The agent, a blue-eyed Greek called Koletsos, jogged back and forth between us and the vendors who remained inside the house: '*He'd sell. It's his wife.*' Dad refused to raise, shrugged and turned away. So we lost. My sister drove away to Kew. I trailed him back to the car. 'Don't worry, Miss,' he said. 'They'll be in touch. My bids were the only two genuine ones they had.' *How could he tell?* 'What'll I say if they ring?' 'Push the faults forward at 'em. The rotten roof on that loose-box. The kitchen. The bathroom.'

———

I cook dinner for M and serve it. 'To think that this time last year I had a broken heart. Do you remember how we used to eat together and play Aretha Franklin records?'

She looks blank, and slightly embarrassed. 'No. I don't remember.'

———

Randolph Stow, *To the Islands*. He wrote it when he was twenty-three. It's a man's book, a young man's book—about the Big Things—death, trying to die, murder, wanting to murder—the land; myth—actually it's brilliant, but there's something grim about it, and deathly serious; he's got no lightness in his personality. There's almost a kind of grinding quality. It's an Important Book. Maybe he's been mad, or something terrible happened to him that crushed all lightness, airiness, wit. Maybe people are born without these.

———

Ran, Kurosawa, with the born-again. As usual in these manly dramas I feel distant and excluded. But a fabulous spectacle.

———

'If you *do* meet someone you like,' says the tough Polish GP, 'for goodness' sake *use condoms*.'

———

I'm supposed to send a story to an anthology. I haven't written a word. I was in that intolerable state of having cleared the decks and finding how far inside me all the real obstacles are. But this morning an hour's work. Two typed pages and the tremulous sense of having hit a vein—that sensation of recognition—as if it were all formal, I mean as if all one were seeking was *form*, and the rest came after.

———

School concert. M played with plenty of attack, rhythm and *feel* the prelude from Bach's Unaccompanied Cello Suite No. 3 in C major. So difficult—she made a lot of mistakes and was white, but there was guts in her playing and I was proud of her.

———

Another ratbag from the seventies comes to visit. 'Remember when—remember how—' His memories of me seem skewed and even invented, though this of course is the Rashomon principle. 'Remember when I told you I went to bed with X *and* Y, the three of us? And you acted not jealous, but for tea you gave me two burnt chops?'

———

When I have begun to carve out the little country of a story in which I will make my home for the next few days (or months, if it should be a novel) I feel a secret power. I don't need to chatter.

———

There's no romance going on with L, just a kind of racketing friendliness. Or maybe it's a smokescreen of shyness.

Darryl Emmerson's *The Pathfinder*—John Shaw Neilson's poems set to music. His sweet tenor, so lovely. Most of the audience was old. I found the story of the poet's life, his lonely struggles, terribly moving. A woman near me pushed up her glasses and wiped her eyes with a shuddering sigh. Her husband saw she was crying and put his arm round her shoulders. Thinking of Neilson's solitariness I wondered if I would be solitary for much of my life from now on, and whether I would find the comfort he did 'in song'.

I dreamt that a man whose beauty was gone—his face had been burnt—brought me a present. I opened it and found first one pigskin glove, then two, as if it had doubled in my hands. They were brown, flexible, seemingly worn in but with the price tag still on them. I slipped my hands into them. They were a perfect fit. The man walked me across a deep meadow, French, high green grass, bordered by a line of poplars.

'I had a dream last night,' said T, 'about cocks. There were three. And I was testing them, to compare and contrast. And the one I chose was the one that went best with its own body.'

At Primrose Gully, a night visitor: a bloke from up the road. Unblinking eyes, ocker manner. Glad not to have been alone when I saw his tall figure stooping to come under the creepers. Q and I tried to hide our boredom, tried to be sociable, while a splendid silver moon rose over the gully and moved steadily up into a cobalt sky through cloudbanks and then wraiths of gossamer. We kept exclaiming; he showed no interest.

A letter from V. Charming, I suppose. He says my handwriting is 'nicely childlike, and yet not'.

———

I read his first novel again. Before I'd heard his voice I never got it, or saw what the fuss was about. It never made me laugh. But now I can hear its tone, and it's so funny that waiting in the foyer of the Con while M does her cello exam I keep giving grunts of laughter and having to sink my mouth into my jumper neck. My response to this is a kind of panic. Why would anyone so brilliant (and giving the appearance of *casual* brilliance) want to have anything to do with *me*?

———

She comes out of the exam all flushed. 'Guess what happened! I had to *sight-read* a Bach *sarabande*! The teacher told me the prelude was all I had to do—but they pointed to the syllabus! And it said "TWO pieces"!' In the evening the teacher rang to apologise. His voice was trembling. I was astonished by his distress. I said, 'Look—she came through it all right. If she'd come home in dark despair maybe I'd feel differently—but she handled it well—and it's the quality of the teaching she's had over the past four years that *enabled* her to handle it.' He seemed relieved, and calmed down. Later she told me about the ambitious mothers of many of the music students: 'They live through their daughters. I *hate* them.'

———

Stomach cramps, attributable only to the fact that L is speeding down the Hume in my direction. I'm jumpy, I can't hide it. I'm a free woman. He's a free man. I like him. He likes me. What am I complaining about?

———

I wake up early to get M off to school. When I return L is sleeping soundly—'sweetly', I think, looking at his head of brown curls half buried in the yellow sheet. I stand by the door and watch him with that respect one feels for completely silent, still slumber.

———

'God,' says the law student, 'he's a hunk, that guy. I saw him coming out of the bathroom'—he makes a two-handed gesture from shoulder to waist—'and I wanted to say, "You can be in my video clip! You can mime *my* part!"'

———

I manoeuvre the complicated intersections that lead off the Westgate Bridge and listen with a burning curiosity to L's tale of heartbreak. 'I can't even use her name! I've had a terrible year. Probably the worst year of my life. Thousands of dollars worth of phone calls. Always rushing from one country to another. The strain of everything. The language problem. The only happiness I've had this year's been with you.'

I look up sharply. *Me?* Have I got the dates wrong?

He's addicted to drama, glamour, pain. He's almost totally un-self-examined, at least in the sense in which I mean it.

———

I sneaked a look in his address book when he was out of the room. There she was. I had expected beauty but was shocked by what I saw in her face: a delicacy of emotional tone that was almost frightening. Wide face, wide-set eyes, an enormous mouth that still looked childlike—it was the mouth that was terrifying—it looked as if it was quivering, the shape of its top lip was irregular in a way that was too sensitive for life. I felt a stab of fear—I mean for *her*—and for him too because he's put what happened in a little shrine, with a candle burning in front of it, and he worships it.

———

He wakes panting from a dream. He's had a phone call. It's her; but her voice fades away and is disconnected—it's a nightmare,

I feel the shock of it, how it hurts him.

I see that I've actually lived a quiet life.

In the restaurant he asks me how my marriage ended. He shudders with horror, picks up a knife and mimes operatically stabbing himself in the heart.

'If something like that happened to me I'd—I'd—I'd never have *seen* them again—I'd have wiped them out of my life! I'd have—'

'You'd have to kill something in yourself, to achieve that. That's revenge. That's useless.'

'But you can't be an emotional *wimp* about it. You've got the right to *feel* things.'

'Are you kidding? Do you think I didn't *feel* anything? I was wounded. I was bleeding.'

With him one can use that sort of language.

He leaves me a Gilberto tape. I play it over and over, in the car. What on earth can come of this? Nothing but the pleasure of what it is. Let it be what it is, then. And be grateful.

———

Deeply embedded in V's novel are turns of phrase of an Australianness I've never before seen on paper. Someone describes a collection of railway stations, of which one was 'completely rusty. The platform, benches, even the ticket office…were all made from old railway track. Passengers would always *come away with orange hands*.' 'Come away with.' This could be my mother speaking. I laugh again and again, and at times shudder at what awfulness he sees in people.

———

Having a beer in the kitchen with the law student while I cook dinner. We talk about falling in love.

'Do you learn how not to,' he asks, 'as you get older?'

'You learn what the process is, and you recognise its stages.'

'Do you mean you can *stop* yourself?'

'You can discipline yourself. You can feel the moment at which it would be possible to let go another string of yourself, and you can choose whether to or not.'

'I've said "I love you" about a thousand times.'

'So have I.'

'*Have* you?'

'Of course,' I said. 'A million times.'

'And I always mean it.'

'Me too. Or—hang on—I've probably had to force it out two or three times.'

'*Force* it out?'

'I mean I said it when it was no longer true. Just to make someone feel all right.'

'I know exactly what you mean. When Donna used to come round here, remember? All I had to do was say "I love you" and she'd stop crying. It was the only thing that'd make her stop.'

Three teenage suicides in the news: a boy hangs himself after an argument about eating too many biscuits; a boy shoots himself because he wasn't allowed to have a motorbike; a sixteen-year-old girl shoots herself with a shotgun and they don't know why. 'Don't anyone out there even *think* of doing it,' said the mother of one of the boys on TV. 'You don't know what you leave behind.'

A sunny day. I am wearing a floppy skirt with hyacinth and white stripes. The psychological effect of wearing stripes. They move, and cross each other, with an audible whirr.

Dreamt I was wheeling my bike towards the uni through an unfinished two-storey building. I was wearing a thin white nightie but also a black jacket that meant I was reasonably modest. Workmen whistled at me but in imitation because I was singing as I went along. In a garden I asked a man, 'How deep is that compost heap?' The compost heap was beautiful. It had a coating of green moss and did not look ugly or messy: it contained a *substance*, it seemed, already smooth and broken down.

———

I thought of volunteering at the Children's Hospital. But there are huge nurses' strikes on.

———

Watching 'experimental' movies is terribly cheering—makes one feel more *daring*.

———

Lying in despair on the couch in my work room I noticed in the wire shelf a forgotten notebook. Pulled it out. It was a sort of diary I had kept back at the beginning of writing *The Children's Bach*. At first I thought, I'll be able to sell this one day. Then I read it and saw with astonishment and relief the HOPELESS MESS my mind was, back then. I thought of the shapely thing *The Children's Bach* is, and remembered that writing a novel is a process of refinement. Out of chaos comes the fine thing; out of chaos comes *form*.

———

In an essay Fay Zwicky quotes Germaine Greer about Henry Handel Richardson's 'provincialism' in being unable to see that *The Getting of Wisdom* is superior to *Maurice Guest*: '…for in a country which is utterly philistine, people who are genuinely excited by the arts tend to distrust any art form which seems close to ordinary life and to adopt paranoid, overblown concepts of the artistic personality'.

———

Worked on the bandaid story, wept over it a bit—it's still lumpy and clumsy, but I am *working* on it.

———

The house vendors have accepted my offer. I signed a contract.

I used the expression 'a beachhead' about the steadiness I've worked out for myself over this year. The Jungian sat up. He quoted Freud—'Where id is, there ego shall be'—and said he thought 'beachhead' was a better image than the strict idea of the ego descending right over the id (he made a covering, seizing movement from above with one claw-like hand). 'The ocean's still there. Nothing's permanently reclaimed. It can all be washed right back in.' He said, 'Now you're back in contact with that part of yourself you'd lost, you must feel reluctant to lose it again in a big projection—which is what falling in love is—letting your whole peace of mind be dependent on someone else.'

My forty-fourth birthday (and La Stupenda's sixtieth, I heard on the radio on my way to the pool). M won't come out with me for breakfast. The law student, embarrassed perhaps, offers himself as company.

I told L my husband gave me a lemon tree for my birthday.
    'A lemon? Sour fruit. Couldn't he have chosen a peach?'

Dreamt I was standing on a bridge over a canal, looking down into the water. A black, hairy, slimy creature surfaced and swam away down the canal. I screamed, 'A rat!' but it was too big to be a rat. I watched with revulsion as it swam away from me, its shoulders working, and then dragged itself up on to the bank. I saw it wasn't a rat, it was as big as a cat and had a thickness at the root of its tail that made it unidentifiable.
    Trigger for this: a dead thing near the tram stop the other day when the law student and I were driving.

HG: 'It's a rat. It's huge.'
LS: 'I don't think it is a rat. Go back, let's have another look.'
U-turn.
HG: 'You're right, it's a baby possum.'

We both made sentimental noises. Whereas when it was a rat we thought, Good riddance.

Clowning with M on the couch, actually having her in my arms and making her laugh by teasing her about the trumpet player in the band, who is six foot three, pale-skinned, handsome, with a WWI face and brow, hair pulled back in a ponytail.

V's piece about Borneo in the *National Times*. An efficient piece of writing without any sign that his emotions had been engaged. And why should they? It's only journalism.

Dreamt my sister and two other women gave me, in a huge cinema, baskets of flowers and herbs to plant in the garden of my new house. In exchange I wrote out for them the words of 'Praise My Soul the King of Heaven'.

Went to work and wrote a short story about a 'luminous boy'. It poured out in a rush and then I spent a timeless couple of hours fiddling with it, changing this and that, cutting, shaping etc— utterly enjoyable. Now I must discipline myself not to spoil it with my cumbersome afterthoughts.

R rang and offered me their house in Sydney for three weeks while they're down the coast.

M came home from her HSC English exam in excellent spirits. Her father called her at dinnertime from America and after this she was radiant with happiness.

―――

A cheque arrived from the lady in Queensland. Stunned, I accepted. I gave half of it to my sister so she could see a shrink.

―――

L sends me an account of his latest struggles to extract himself from emotional entanglements ('you must think I'm a walking basket case'), plus a drawing of his just-planted garden. I wrote back, taking a breezy tone: 'You are much too charming and good-looking for a tranquil life, and in this respect we belong to different species.' Told him I'd be in Sydney in summer. 'But you're overloaded. The last thing you need is more female attention. You sound like a man who's going down for the third time in a sea of consequences.'

―――

Mass-murderers of girls arrested and charged in Perth. A married couple in their thirties. Shallow bush graves. Stranglings, suffocations, sexual assaults. What does this *mean*? The devil, A would say. The rottenness in people.

―――

While M slaves in her room for tomorrow's exam the law student and I drink beer downstairs and listen to Miles Davis and Mink De Ville. I'm fascinated by the power that beauty has over him. 'On the beach, Helen, I'd look at this creation—the *colour* of her, and the skin of her arms—and I'd be nearly passing out—thinking, How can God have made something this *perfect*?'

―――

At Brunswick Baths I was alone for an hour against a brick wall in the sun reading J's new stories in proofs. His terrifying prolificness. I read until I felt trembly, hypoglycaemic, and had to go home.

―――

L grumbles on the phone: 'I watched that show on Brazil—God, why do I live in this country? It's so self-satisfied here. In Brazil there's so much *energy*—' etc etc, ho hum, but underneath is fear: the first draft of his novel is 900 pages long, 'a mess'. He says, 'I was reading *Postcards from Surfers* again the other day and I could see how it's made up of notebook things—it's terrific, how you do that?' I bet he really thinks, She hasn't got an imagination as big and creative as *mine*. Heh heh. Polished up my little story and sent it to the *Adelaide Review*.

———

At the baths I lay on a wonderful foam rubber object I bought en route at K-Mart, fount of all goodness. Creamed my skin, put on my sunglasses, and just as I was about to lie down I glanced towards the northern end of the pool and saw four people, a group, of different sizes and ages, sitting on the rim. Something in their postures, their groupness, the angles of their spines filled me with a rush of bliss so intense that my eyes ran with tears. How could I have forgotten this *simple joy*? Available to any moron with the money to get past the turnstile. The sky was pure blue, and in it sailed great galleons of cloud, white with blue-grey floors. I felt my skin begin to burn. I swam a length in the cold water, shuddering, in my goggles. Two rough girls near me kept giving me friendly looks and smiles. God, I was happy, I was content!

———

I'm shortlisted for the *Age* book of the year, which I have never won or even, I think, been shortlisted for. I look at the list of judges and think, I haven't won. I feel nothing. I determine not to go to the presentation. Never again, that shameful public torment.

———

Dancing in Lygon Street to Venetta Fields and her band—the wonderful power of gospel, its shouts of joy. Five minutes of that music does more to convert a person than six months of solemnity from a born-again in your house. Just before the last song she said, 'That lady in the blue dress who's been clappin' and singin'—maybe you'll know this song—"Steal Away to Jesus!"' People looked around. She meant *me*. I blushed. Two men dancing—Aussie crim types—one a stumpy pale little fellow with very muscly legs bared by rude torn-off denim shorts, the other tall and limp-backed in a Hawthorn beanie and cheap fawn trousers. They seemed to know each other and danced in a way that was distressing—tensely, with clenched arms and bent knees and no fluidity of spine, all aggression. A black American danced right in front of me, a great hunk of a man with massive hips, bum, thighs—his relaxed authority—nothing flashy or even skilful, just easy in his body and glad to be moving. Everything he did originated in his hips, completely centred there and at ease.

Roland Barthes, in *A Lover's Discourse*, on dedicating a book: 'Writing is dry, obtuse; a kind of steamroller, writing advances, indifferent, indelicate, and would kill "father, mother, lover" rather than deviate from its fatality (enigmatic though that fatality may be). When I write, I must acknowledge this fact...: there is no benevolence within writing, rather a terror: it smothers the other, who, far from perceiving the gift in it, reads there instead an assertion of mastery, of power, of pleasure, of solitude. Whence the cruel paradox of the dedication: I seek at all costs to give you what smothers you.'

Hmmm. I see it's a proper noting and working out of the tiniest flickers of consciousness, a teasing out of their meanings i.e. (like Handke) he is using the same raw material that I use, and his field of operation is home to me, but we perform different acts/actions upon it.

I wonder if I will become one of those women in their forties who have affairs with married men. No! I will not. Full of curiosity about this one, though—V. I read an interview with him and see his alarming statements and concerns—how he is 'horrified' by the idea of the 'erosion of his standards'. This is real, stern, rigid animus talking. But I can't say he hasn't warned me—describing his own hand-writing as 'cramped, tight, stilted and jerky, and this nib can't be blamed'.

―――

The *Adelaide Review* paid me $200 for my story. Now I'm working on the opera one. Something improves in it every day, and I get more control over it. Today I fiddled with the river and water imagery.

―――

Meeting at the Windsor about some film festival I'm invited to. Two cups of tea and a glass of orange juice cost *$11*. We nearly fainted.

―――

A critic, writing about Elizabeth Jolley: 'Compared to Garner, who was once presented to us as the *enfant terrible* of Australian fiction—'

―――

Reading Elizabeth Bowen, very good of course in an infuriating English way. Full of depths, if not widths.

―――

Three mothers of teenagers laughing together at the dinner table. Two of us talk about how sexy the son of the third one is. I jokingly offer to take him to live at my place. 'Take him,' she says. 'I bet he'd be the perfect gentleman at your place. To me he says "Fuck up and die."'

―――

I spent an hour standing on a high stool at the cupboard reading old diaries. My bare feet were blue with cold. Pain of those years, when I read them without the filter of previous ignorance. Why didn't I see that the marriage was already done for? The soul was not itself.

———

A woman's tinkling showers of laughter.

———

Dad came to Primrose Gully, taught me to use the motor mower. A wheel came off, twice, and he showed me how to fix it with a piece of wire. I was impressed with his competence, patience and ability to improvise. He went home. I cut the grass on my own. Now I understand why he used to be so single-minded about it. It's positive destruction. You're obsessed, walled in by the tremendous noise, faced with a design problem—the pattern of the strokes. You can't hear voices speaking to you, the phone has no hope of being heard, you have the luxury of being incommunicado. You see an immediate result. After mowing, I raked.

———

The native tree outside our back gate is thickly covered in cream-coloured flowers. The street is lined with these trees, but none of the others has more than half a dozen blossoms. Ours is the only one that is riotously flourishing. The law student and I noticed this on our way back from the shop. I said, 'It must be because we have such a happy household.'

———

The law student has found a room in a student house and will leave in ten days.

———

'I've got many *things*,' says L. He wants to show me his life. His sweet-smelling skin, his thick curls. The bedroom is in the very centre of his house. The streetlight is blocked by curtains. We make love in pitch blackness. He is generous with the bed: leaves plenty of room for me. We sleep, or rather he sleeps, and I drift all night just below the surface, with occasional brief dives deeper.

———

'They arrested a bloke in Brisbane who had a bomb to blow up the Pope. He was from a lunatic asylum.'

'Was he making *purposeful strides* towards the Pope?'

We fall about at this but she was not trying to amuse.

———

'I love talking to girls,' says the law student. 'I *need* to. I feel as if I need to release something in me.'

———

At the lunch table I can't help staring at V, the married man. I want to let my eyes wander freely. A plain man. A very white neck. Old, soft, faded Levi shirt, jeans, horrible old seventies boots with heels, black corduroy jacket. He's the flipside of L, the curly-headed, laughing one. He is very *male*. Something very definite and uncompromising about him. Do I mean 'rigid and inflexible'? I don't know, yet.

———

At Toki I tell the law student about the two men. He listens with bated breath, groans and shouts. When I start to *compare* them he twists in his chair and cries out as if in pain.

———

The law student stumbles in after a night at a party and the Users' Club. 'This guy called Daniel says to me, "Hey! Come upstairs! There's this fabulous guitar!" So I go up to a bedroom and we play this steel-string guitar, and he plays some blues and I play some blues, and I show off; and whenever I do anything on the guitar that I—see, he's not very *musical*—he's a really nice guy but he—so if I do something that I just *feel*, he says, "Oh! How'd you do that? Show me! I wanna learn! I wanna learn!" And I feel like saying, "Go and listen to this record. *I* can't teach you."'

L took me to his friends' house for lunch. We sat at the table in the sun, drinking and talking *as people do*. We all got on merrily. I sat beside him, liking him and liking everything. I saw his lovely sociability, his readiness. When people spoke he listened, and when it was his turn he spoke. One of the women was very pregnant. The pure skin of pregnancy. Her dainty ankles and sparkling eyes. I felt very drawn to her, wanted to stroke and pat her and admire her radiance, and I did.

After dinner the waiter brought L the wrong coffee, was corrected, went away. Time passed. He realised he'd been forgotten and from that moment the evening was lost. He went dark and stiff with rage. Anger spread into the air around him. A grille clanged down between him and the world. I panicked. All the air went out of me. I felt my face drop on its bones. He noticed and said, 'What's up?' I said, in a small voice, 'I feel sad. And scared.' 'Sorry,' he said, 'I just hate it when things like that happen, when people treat you like—' I wanted to say, 'He doesn't scorn you, or hate you—he just made a mistake.' But his whole ego was bound up in it. My own iron grille came down. I missed the chance to level with him. From then on we were both deep in reticence but keeping the superficial intimacy going. In the morning, a shyness. I like him. I envy his beauty and I hate the way it distorts his life. He is all split and troubled; and his loneliness is as bad as mine. We would wear each other out.

'You can feel Patrick White in your own writing, can't you,' says the man. 'Sometimes you look at a sentence and you can see where it comes from—completely unconsciously. That's his power.'

'Yes,' says the woman gaily, 'even in someone like me who's hardly even *read* him.'

―――

Two actors walk into Pellegrini's, the wife more famous and highly regarded than the husband. He walks very close behind her, shepherding her through the crowd, chin high and wearing the look that says, 'I am famous and I am only looking at you for two reasons: (1) to check briefly whether I shall greet you if by chance you too are famous and (2) to repel your eager glance if you are not.' Her skin is white white *white*: the whiteness (1) of the redhead and (2) that says 'I work indoors', bounces back light and makes her photogenic.

―――

Outside the university college, in the dark garden, a huge magnolia tree held out its opening buds, and in the street some night birds were singing, one in one tree, one in another. I remembered a French essay I wrote in 1961 about those birds, which I heard near the Union sandwich bar on an early summer night just before my first uni exams.

―――

I dreamt that my nutty old boyfriend from the other side of the river was near me, singing sweetly.

―――

I stood.
   'Why do you have to go now?' said V.
   'Because I have to do something in Melbourne at six o'clock.'
We were looking each other right in the eyes. Not a romantic or soft look, but a direct, hard challenge, straight out of the hard self.

―――

P walked with me at Primrose Gully. We took sticks against snakes. Grass very long, with beautiful russet tips.

―――

I dreamt of a yellow object. I forget what it was. Was it thickly coated in perfect duco? About the size of—what? Even that's gone.

It gleamed, it was bright, smooth, it made the heart glad.

———

At the launch the writer kissed me on the cheek and gave me a cassette of her work. Her bright make-up, narrow fox-like face, her straw-dyed and square-chopped hair, and a little black fez.

———

Damn it. There's an opening in me towards where V is. If we lived in the same town I would write and say, 'Tonight, grave sir, both my poore house, and I,/ Do equally desire your companie…' —Ben Jonson, *Inviting a Friend to Supper*

———

After I'd signed a paper agreeing to pay the house loan back 'on demand' should anything 'go wrong', Dad became expansive and made orotund pronouncements on matters of family finance, saying each thing several times in several different ways. We had steak, perfect boiled potatoes, peas they'd picked at Portarlington, and strawberries ditto, with King Island cream. A fabulous, classic lunch in our mother's tradition. He put a spoonful of tomato sugo on my steak, reaching over my shoulder with a flourish deft enough to get him a job at the Italian Society. Driving home with my brother: warm wind, the huge, low horizon of that plain, streaks of grey cloud and a hot-looking sunset.

———

On the phone Y and I went through my story line by line and raked all the lumps out of it, cut off the last sentence, fixed misleading punctuation etc. Of course I'm anxious about it. Is she really telling the truth when she says it's 'lovely' and 'fine' and that she 'loves' it?

———

Speech Night. Hundreds of brown-legged girls in those ugly, bag-like uniforms. Nothing can make a young girl less than lovely. The steadiest, quietest, most faithful, least ambitious, least flamboyant thing in the world is the alto voice in a girls' madrigal group. The law student and I whisper across each other, 'It's so *quiet*.' 'It's so *calm*.' When the choir sings an Elgar song, 'The Snow', with two violins, a father on my other side cries openly, tears collecting in the creases under his eyes; then, between items, he opens a business magazine and reads on. *'C'était un peu sucré,'* says F. The law student and I, both tear-stained, are pained by his refusal *'d'être ému'*. A professor of economics gives a rousing feminist speech: 'It's all out there waiting for you—you can have a *wonderful life*.' On the way home I mention this admiringly. M is less impressed: 'We get told that kind of stuff every week at assembly.'

———

The man's clothes are very expensive, and look it—suits obviously Italian, shoes of the fashionable clod-hopper kind. His ex-wife's are well-chosen, stylish, fashionable, but when seen close up are of cheap cut and material. She puts her money elsewhere, I guess. She is potentially beautiful. What stops her is unhappiness, anger, resentment.

———

Dreamt I was a police cadet. I was lonely and a bit scared in the building where we were being trained. I made friends with a young bloke, not my type at all, curly-haired and beefy, not all that bright. We were issued with a kind of yearbook, containing a page about each of us. My page said that he was my friend and I was embarrassed.

———

L wants worldly esteem. I know that feeling. I hope he'll get it because it means so much to him that if he doesn't it will deflate him and make him sad and bitter.

———

What am I setting up for myself, here? Some happiness, perhaps.

I'm calm, and in good spirits, quietly, as if something important and good were about to happen. I'm not scared or nervous. I can't even imagine it, how it will be, what it will look like, what felicities or clumsinesses either of us will commit. Bucket of cold water: he's married. He is an intellectual and *I am not*. 'He lives,' said Z, who introduced us, 'almost entirely in the world of books and ideas. I imagine that's why he didn't want to have children.' Maybe he's in the habit of having quick, harsh, demanding affairs. Or maybe this will be an important relationship, for both of us.

———

At the peace vigil a pastor gets up and says, 'The most important thing I've written in the last year is some remarks I made at a meeting about trying to re-unite North and South Korea. You'll hear the emotion and the politics in it.' He then proceeds to read, in a wooden voice, an interminable sermon. He stood with his heels together and his feet in a broad V. At the end he said, 'Amen.'

———

Went to Borsari's and bought a new bike, a Puch 5-speed, big and female and reliable as a pram. With girl's handlebars and a skirt guard. Flew home up Lygon Street, sitting up with straight back, not angled forward as on the too-racy Hillman which I now pass on to M.

———

At Heide I liked the paintings very much. Arthur Boyd bridegroom pictures. Bouquets sprouting from people's ears. In a frame, several pages torn from the artist's notebook, from the early fifties, pencil scribbles on yellowing paper. He can't spell at all—very endearing. '*Cresent moon always looks like this…dingoe's sniffing bone's.*'

———

The enclosed garden, full of flowers, very beautiful. V is botanically even more ignorant than I am. At the bottom of it an extraordinary vegetable—is it a turnip? A betterave like on the French kitchen poster? It's mauve and green, as big as a canteloupe, touches the earth on a lower point, and is held vertical by flying buttresses of long, muscular-looking leaves. It is split, and looks dry and woody inside.

———

V doesn't like his name. 'Why don't you change it?' 'If you change your name you have to change your surname as well, don't you? 'Cause that's what you *are*.' 'Most women change their surnames at least once in their lives.' He's surprised—never thought of this before.

———

In the warm and windy night streets, kids stumble about in gangs or alone. A chubby girl carrying her shoes and smoking stops me and asks me the time.

'Five to eleven.'

'Oh! I thought it was later.'

Her face is smeared, somehow—she is drunk and unhappy, perhaps has been humiliated. She tries to smile at me. Her features aren't anchored in place, they slide on her face. I feel a pang for her. She stumbles away up Russell Street.

V says, 'Why's she got her shoes off and her shirt hanging out?'

"Cause she's unhappy, and her feet hurt 'cause she's a fat girl. And some man's probably just been cruel to her.'

'For sure. At the bottom of every bit of trouble there's always a man.'

'Yes. You only have to look, and there is.'

This banter, which to me is flippant, is perhaps less so to him.

He presses: 'Do you think that's true?'

'Oh, I don't know.'

'See, I think what women don't realise is that men like to be with other men.'

'That shouldn't cause problems necessarily, should it?'

All evening I am dodging and feinting, to avoid being pinned down.

———

'What did you do in the fifties?'

'Lay on my bed and read. Listened to Little Richard records and danced. Mucked around with my family. What did you?'

'Cars,' says V. 'I was crazy about speed. I drove an MG, stripped down, no floor.'

'Where'd you put your feet?'

'Well, there was a *bit* of floor, on the driving side. But in the rest you could see the ground going past.'

———

Me: 'What's your house like?'

V: 'You should come there one day.'

Me: (*thinks*) 'What? Don't be ridiculous.'

———

'You know how marvellous it is,' says the woman in Notturno, 'to be with another writer. They don't get bored or think you're mad.' But this stuff I'm writing in here will embarrass me later when V ceases to be a MYSTERIOUS STRANGER and reveals all his meanness and weakness (and I mine).

———

Thelonious Monk playing 'Ruby My Dear'. Over and over. On the cover: 'He had evolved an unorthodox approach to the piano, involving crushed notes and clusters, and left-hand chords made up of seconds and sixths instead of conventional triadic jazz harmonies.' They're only technical terms but I wish I'd made up 'crushed notes and clusters'.

———

V turned away from me, while we were looking in a shop window, and I caught a whiff of him—only faint—but it was a *plain* smell, unadorned and unperfumed (not like that of L, who's all fresh and herbal)—a smell of wool, of ordinary skin—*not young*—a smell that reminded me of my father and *my grandfather*—I was jolted by the connection—and I thought, If I do know you when you are old, it will have been a plain life indeed.

———

Gloomily coming into my bedroom I stump towards the bed and see the mess of *New York Reviews* beside it, and a copy of Joan London's stories that are so beautiful, and I think, Whatever happens, I've got this one little *power*—I'm a writer. I can use everything that happens, I can use it and shape it and in that way I can get control of it.

———

It has been discovered that humans emit certain smells or substances which cause *health* in the opposite sex. Men can only pass on their health-giving substances by sex. Women's, however, can be conveyed over distance and even tend to permeate the atmosphere—and women's, also, work on other women. *Really?*

———

I see that what I am doing, in this diary, is conducting an argument with myself, about these two men, and myself, and men in general.

———

Family lunch at the Latin. Just as my sister is getting red-faced and shrill about the nurses' strike, two men rush through the room, one cringing under the blows of the other who is covered in a white mess of food and roaring in a fury: 'How *dare* you! You're only a waiter!' They roll on to the street and disappear. 'You can tell it's a joke,' says my sister, 'because he said, "How *dare* you?" No Australian would say that. He'd say, "You bastard!" and punch him in the face.' 'Aww, I dunno,' says our father. 'I reckon if one of 'em had had a knife there'da been real trouble.'

In the shack I get up to take the kettle off the fire and see through the narrow window a pretty sight: a blue wren flirting with his own reflection in the outside mirror of my car. He flips up, whirring his wings like mad, performs a caracole and a pirouette in mid-air before the glass, then perches on the mirror's rim and looks around in confusion—then back he goes and does it all again.

'Most people are not aware of such a call' (to the numinous) 'yet they may feel the strongest attraction to make some sense of the "God-feeling" within them, and be overwhelmed by feelings of sickness, sadness, depression and despair if they suppress it because they disagree with conventional kinds of religious belief, or are afraid that others will think them mad or odd...They will find it painful to begin with to admit to being driven by such an improper longing, but if they can get past this stage they will discover that most people have a very good idea what they are talking about and are repressing similar longings and experiences of their own...We are all contemplatives to a greater or lesser degree, and we all need, to the limit of our capacity, to admit the experience which we may, or may not, call God.' —Monica Furlong, *Contemplating Now*

All this is true, and it is what my novel should be about. The spirit comes to an unhappy woman. She denies it. It departs. I'm frightened of all this, I think.

Fear—of being drawn to another man whose phlegmatic nature will limit and distort mine—or for whose sake I will limit and distort *myself*. And yet I am so much stronger, now.

The only way I can have anything to do with him is by (a) lies and (b) hurting someone. Am I prepared to do this?

———

Annie Gottlieb's dream that when she began to enjoy her 'powers as a writer', her mother had her sterilised. The terrific jolt of this: *I didn't simply dream being sterilised*. In the year between the writing of *Monkey Grip* and its publication, I had it done to myself.

———

The university year ends. Our law student is moving out.
    Me: 'How will I live without you?'
    Him: 'Who'll I talk to?'

———

'There are virtually,' says V, 'only two things that go wrong with a car engine. Petrol, or—far more likely—spark.'

———

The window is open, the curtains lift and drop on a warm breeze that smells strongly of dry grass.

———

Went and had a little haircut. I think the hairdresser's freaking out. He cut it dry, a thing he's never done before. He was late. He looked pale, distracted; is going to France on Thursday. Has moved out of his house and is sleeping in the salon.

———

The biographer talks about her progress. 'I didn't *want* to write another book about a put-upon woman. At first I was full of admiration for her. I thought she was a heroine. Then I saw what really happened, and I was angry. And then I sulked.' She gives her tuneful laugh. 'Yes—I *sulked*. And now I know that if it *has* to be a book about an oppressed woman, that's what it'll be.'

———

Because I know that someone finds 'almost everything about' me 'interesting', I am walking round in a cloud of power.

In an old diary I find this exchange between me and Y:

Me: 'I'd like to have a man in another city. I'd like him to be crazy about me, and for him to write me wonderful letters, once or twice a week, and to come to me every now and then, and me to him—a real passion—but for him not to want to make me his wife.'

Y: 'Now you're talking.'

I forgot to mention that *I* would like also to be crazy about *him*.

Invited to eat with two high-powered academics, philosophers. I'm happily surprised by their worldliness. While she works in the kitchen she has the radio on low and I hear her singing along to the Bangles: 'Walk like an Egyp-she-an.' She tells a tale of drunkenness, of 'calling for a bucket'. Feel no longer shy of asking them what, for example, Heidegger was on about. Rain fell, quiet and vertical, at dinner.

A letter I can't quite bring myself to write to L:

'I'm no good at these reticent, half-hearted affairs. I thought for a while it was what I needed, in my awkward, bruised convalescence; and because you seemed to be in a similar state I felt it all to be appropriate. But I feel your wariness and it's brought out all my own: it made me grow a thicker skin. And now you're on the outside of it and voilà.'

If I told the whole truth I would have to say: 'I think I've fallen in love with someone else.'

A woman has reviewed *Postcards from Surfers* and *The Children's Bach* in the *New York Times Book Review*: '...lit by a kind of eerie, slanted light, reminiscent at times of Jane Bowles's work, as are

Ms Garner's sharp, strange images and the dense, rich texture their layering creates.'

I know it's dangerous to dwell on praise but allow me a little moment of delight at being mentioned in the same sentence as Jane Bowles.

———

I am mean to our dog. I ignore her when she casts herself at my feet. I must be in love.

———

Dreamt I sat on a couch beside another person, a cheerful man I knew to be a semi-reformed crim. From the floor a dog, hairy and importunate, wormed its way between us. We went to a strange house, where in a derelict room with no furniture a fire was only just alight in a big, empty fireplace. While I waited for him to come into this room (were we going to make love?) I took the poker and moved the fire around, grouped its fallen parts and tried to make it burn properly. There was no wood, the room was quite empty and dark, and the fire was almost ashes, but still gave out a little bit of warmth if not a clear flame.

———

Sun came out of the clouds while I was in the pool. Water suddenly full of little yellow feathers.

———

The Polish philosopher said she had found Stendhal's *On Love* attractive and relevant 'as an adolescent', but that now she considers love to be 'a cancer of the mind—you pick a man out of the crowd, and you demand that he should play a part, that he should be this, and that—it's grotesque! It's ridiculous!' I came away rather sobered. Fortunately I was *en vélo* and this always cheers me up in doubtful moments.

———

An Italian photographer from a magazine. He reminded me of the one who said to me meanly in the seventies, 'Your profile, it is not the best.' But this one ended up charming me into smiling and laughing. He even laid his palm against my cheek.

———

'All the kids in maximum security,' says the poet, 'have read your book. And they *love* it.' Am I supposed to believe this? His alarming gaze. He can fix you for up to five minutes without blinking. Is that a jail thing? His hard, forceful presence, his hard talk and anecdotes, his need to *keep talking*, his discourse of violence—what he said to men who crossed him, what he said he'd do to them, what he in fact *did* do to them. 'I jumped up and down on his arm, I was yellin', "Ya cunt, if you break *her* arm I'm gunna break yours."' I kept thinking, must I take account of this? Is it *middle class* not to want to? 'I was bored with m' wife,' he says. 'I kept saying, "Here, go and buy yourself a nice dress or something." But she wouldn't. She'd wear a tracksuit, 'n' ugg boots.'

———

Out all day with the jaws of my purse straining wide. Horror of Christmas. But I exchanged friendly looks with many strangers…I like people when they are in a great mass, thousands of lonely or rather solitary blobs, each one with '*le front barré de souci*'.

———

The barrier of shyness that attacks us both (and especially V) when we're together. I mean sexual shyness. As if we were learning each other by some more decorous means. An inversion of the modern order.

———

One day I'll have to burn this book. I use as buckets of cold water thoughts of his wife's preparations for Christmas.

———

The landlord comes to examine the cracked wall and the powerful wisteria on the house-front. F is visiting. I set up the ironing board and say to the girls, 'Sing to us.' One plays the piano, the other sings: *An die Musik*. While I work, F sits quite still with his forearms on the table. I don't dare look at him; it's a song that brings such painful memories of the music we discovered together. *'Du holde Kunst, in wieviel grauen Stunden…'* They sing other less poignant songs, and shift into carols. We join in. Meanwhile the landlord wanders up and down the stairs. I pass him in the hall. He's standing still, listening to the girls' voices: 'Isn't it lovely!' Later, in the kitchen, he tells me a story: 'When I was a kid I had a really good voice. I sang all the time, in choirs. I was good, and I loved it. My father—he was a wonderful man—used to get me to sing for him when we were going along together in the car. Then one day I overheard him talking to another bloke, someone he knew, a neighbour or someone he worked with. He was saying, "Some blokes have sons who are footballers. Some have sons who are runners. But I've got a son who's a singer." I thought he was ashamed of me. So I stopped. Gave it up. Never sang again. And years later he said to me, "I've never understood, John—why'd you stop singing?"'

On the doorstep he pauses. It will be fine with him, he says, if the four girls live here when I move out.

Maybe he's the kind of man who conducts flirtations with women in such a way as to allow his wife to find out; she then puts a stop to the developing affair and, though he grumbles etc, *this is what he wants, and needs*. No idea why I thought of this. Just running through the painful possibilities.

On TV a dramatised life of Freud. Very enjoyable. Did he really have a black lower lip, like a dog's? The madwomen in the hospital:

raving, twitching, and nothing that could be done.

———

'You look well. You look happy. Are you?'
  'Yes, I am happy.' Feeling my flesh light on my bones.

———

The visiting German editor wants me to write a big piece about Melbourne. Though his monthly circulation is 250,000 he offers me only $1200. I make a series of small sounds meant to indicate slight interest in the piece but lack of excitement about the money. We agree to write to each other. Before my foot hits the pavement outside I have lost interest.

———

'I'm a woman now,' says M, pirouetting at the kitchen door.
  'How do you mean?'
  'I got my learner's permit. I'm allowed to drive a car. *I* can *drive* a *car*.'
  We laugh so madly we have to lean on the walls. Fact: I love her more than anyone in the world.

———

Whenever I start worrying about not being beautiful and young, I try to imagine a man of my age, someone whose age shows, who is not glamorous, who's got wrinkles, but who's got a sexual presence and an authority of personality. I imagine him in a group of people, sitting there quietly, not making a fuss. And I think, if *he* can be attractive, *so can I*.

———

In the car with F and M, last night, tired and crabby, I began to see my secret new fantasies as silly and pointless. How long does it take two people to slide into *being a couple*? But then F gave me a garden spade for Christmas. In my fatigue I had forgotten all the nice and lovely things about him, how funny he is, how on the drive home (he drove) we sang together, with M, for miles.

———

A two-year-old girl has been stolen from her bed (the person cut through a flywire screen) and 'sexually assaulted'. She was found 'crying and wandering' in a street ten kilometres away at 1 am. Doctors have had to operate on her to repair 'internal injuries'.

———

Cried and bawled by myself in front of the Mediaeval Mystery Plays on TV. Abraham and Isaac, what a terrible story, it made me hate God, the jealous God who demands appalling tributes, but then at the end when he tells Abraham he may spare his son, and says, '*I* am going to sacrifice *my* son, later on,' I was pulled up short.

———

Mum brought to Christmas dinner some very old photos of us four girls as kids, outside the house at Ocean Grove. I saw myself at nine or ten looking so tragically plain that I lost heart for twenty minutes. Dad picked out the one who in the photos looked the most 'cute' and 'timid', then showered her with affection for the entire day. The rest of us craned sideways from a couch in the next room to watch him hold her, with his arm around her waist, while she stood beside his chair. Later she came up to us and said, 'I think Dad loves me.' We went into convulsions of embarrassed laughter.

———

T mended my pink trousers and then we lay on her bed and sofa and shrieked about fucking young or boring men. She fancies a bloke in a pub where she goes to play music. I said, 'Is he a murderer?' 'I don't know,' she said. 'He's boring and has no sense of humour. But every time I see him I feel all stirred up on the way home.'

———

Dreamt that somebody had a baby but it died. A great deal of sobbing. The father was terribly distressed. I was trying to be of use but did not know how. In a paved courtyard I lit a fire in a metal container with a lid. Smoke poured out of it and I went back into the house and forgot about it.

———

Looking around this room I realise I'll only be sleeping in it two or three more times.

1987

A hot, dry day on the Hume, a sky full of detailed, small clouds. Saw two or three dead wombats, a couple of dead kangaroos, and a live brown bird on the gravel with half a dozen live brown chicks. In the dunny at Tarcutta a Vietnamese woman was washing a baby's trousers in the basin. I smiled at her. She said, 'How—to Sydney—how many?' 'Four hours.' *'Four hours!* Very far!' She showed me the child's clothes, made a spewing gesture: 'My boy—*vomit*.' I entertained myself with songs and sexual fantasies. What will become of me? What if he's already thought better of it? Important: *do not wait*. Flying through an outer suburb of Sydney I saw a boy crouched on the footpath with one hand on the side of a dog that had apparently been hit by a car: the boy turned up his face to a standing man. A car was stopped at the kerb. The sheepdog, glossy, long-haired, brownish-yellow, was panting violently, its tongue lolling right out. Oddly matter-of-fact expression on the boy's face. I may have misread the situation.

Leaves working hard in a coolish wind. Nobody in Sydney knows I'm here. There is no food in this borrowed house and I'm not hungry. How lucky I am to be a grown-up (or trying to stay one) in an empty house in another town. I could go somewhere, or visit someone, or call one or both of the men, but I don't want to lose this period of non-existence. Incognito, incommunicado. I feel powerful. As soon as I announce myself my freedom will be over.

———

I'm thinner. Dressing, I see muscles move in my shoulders and upper arms. Swimmer's muscles.

———

In Bernard Crick's life of George Orwell (about Cyril Connolly? Or did Connolly say it about Orwell?): 'And he was emotionally independent with the egoism of all natural writers…'

———

Dreamt of a battered house, a central bedroom with doors opening off it in all directions. The room was dirty, dusty, papers strewn about. Other people and I were busily cleaning it and putting it in order. Someone had tucked a clean white sheet very tightly over a pile of different-sized mattresses, so that what looked orderly was in fact chaotic. I had to take it apart and start again. No resentment—rather an excited happiness at the enterprise of it all.

———

In L's backyard. His tanned face, his habit of smiling and laughing. He talked at length, vehemently, about his annoyance with friends, especially couples with children, who took the liberty of asking him close personal questions of a patronising kind. I wasn't sure what he was getting at. I sat there squinting with my hands around my face against the sun and listened. I pieced together a subtext: that he is still deep in at least one unresolved relationship with a woman. His friends are urging him to choose.

I put my arm round his shoulders (two holes in the top seam of his white T-shirt). '*Do* you want children? Are you going to have children?'

He looks down, shifts in his seat. And it hits me that I'm a protection for him, against a full-on relationship that might lead to his *getting married*. He tells me his father saw his fear of it and said, 'Sooner or later you have to touch that hot thing, and see what happens.'

I felt like saying, Marry someone. Have some kids. I should have said, In my life you are a happy sub-plot. But I only said, 'Don't choose me!'

We laughed.

'You're calm, aren't you,' he said. 'How did you get like that?'

'I'm older.'

'Not that much.'

'Enough. I got sick of being ratty.'

'It'd be ridiculous, at fifty.'

(*Thinks*) 'It'll be ridiculous at forty, baby. You've got two years.' (*says*) 'Also, I've spent a year on my own.'

But I don't think he heard this, the most important bit.

———

The other one calls. His terrifying dry voice. Almost a drawl. I feel shy, almost rebuffed, awkward. I don't know if I can handle this.

We sit under the trees in the garden of the borrowed house. He puts his sunglasses on the table and the wind is so strong that they move across its surface. He says the proofs of his novel have come, and they make him feel sick. We make the kind of conversation about nothing that clever people make when they are too shy to be silent. In the living room I point out some large patches of mould: 'If you had a wall like this in your house, you'd do something about it, wouldn't you.' 'Yes. But I can't help admiring the fact that they don't. Pretty soon that surface is gonna look like expensive French wallpaper. Brocade.'

———

In the gallery he shows me 'the best picture here, maybe the best picture ever painted in Australia'. 'The Sisters', by Hugh Ramsay. 'Why is it the best?' 'Oh, because it's so funny. Because...' He trails off. He shows me a Picasso. It means nothing. I fall behind. Then I pull myself together, detach myself from him, begin to look for myself. 'See this guy?' he says. 'He made his own teeth. Out of wood. His wife used to wear long white gloves. Even in summer. Did you know Lloyd Rees' mother was a leper?'

———

We notice a woman gardener, young and slim with brown legs, shorts, a thick bob, a regulation-issue broad-brimmed hat. An old Chinese woman in a pink, soft, pleated dress, slip-on wedgies and little white socks passes, and we admire her as well.

———

'Can you cook?'

He is astonished: *'Course* not.'

———

On New Year's Eve I call home. 'You should see the dining-room table!' says M, her voice bright with excitement and happiness. 'There's at least twenty-five beer cans on it!'

———

Coming away, with my friends, from the terrible play at the Opera House. The air by the water was creamy. This wonderful city. Every night here, when I turn out the light in my borrowed house, I put on Glenn Gould playing the French Suites and fall happily to sleep, hearing their beauty, intricacy and order.

———

The monolith of his marriage, and my own solitariness and flimsiness by comparison. I feel very small, slight, impermanent. It is not too late for me to save myself.